Wealth Compounded

Wealth Compounded

Strategies for a Secure, Consistent,
and Predicable Retirement Lifestyle...
No Matter What the Stock Market Does

JOSHUA SCHLINSKY

Wealth Compounded

ISBN: 978-0-692-11872-6

Printed in the United States of America Year of First Printing: 2018

Cover Design by: Ken Wilcox

Disclaimer

While great efforts have been taken to provide accurate and current information regarding the covered material, neither Safe Secure Financial nor Joshua Schlinsky are responsible for any errors or omissions, or for the results obtained from the use of this information.

The title, "Wealth Compounded," is a marketing concept and does not guarantee or imply that you will become wealthy. The act of purchasing any book, course, or financial product holds no such guarantees.

The ideas, suggestions, general principles, and conclusions presented here are subject to local, state and federal laws and regulations, and revisions of same, and are intended for informational purposes only. All information in this report is provided "as is" with no guarantee of completeness, accuracy, or timeliness regarding the results obtained from the use of this information and without warranty of any kind, express or implied, including, but not limited to, warranties of performance, merchantability, and fitness for a particular purpose. Your use of this information is at your own risk.

You assume full responsibility and risk of loss resulting from the use of this information. Joshua Schlinsky and Safe Secure Financial is not liable for any direct, special, indirect, incidental, consequential, or punitive damages or any other damages whatsoever, whether in an action based upon a statute, contract, tort (including, but not limited to negligence), or otherwise, relating to the use of this information.

In no event will Joshua Schlinsky, Safe Secure Financial, or their related partnerships or corporations, or the partners, agents, or employees of Joshua Schlinsky or Safe Secure Financial be liable to you or anyone else for any decision made or action taken in reliance on the information in this book or for any consequential, special, or similar damages, even if advised of the possibility of such damages.

Neither Joshua Schlinsky nor Safe Secure Financial are engaged in rendering legal, accounting, or other professional services. If accounting, financial, legal, or tax advice is required, the services of a competent professional should be sought.

Facts and information in this book are believed to be accurate at the time of publication and may become outdated by marketplace changes or conditions, new or revised laws, or other circumstances. All figures and examples in this report are based on rates and assumptions no later in time than May 2018. Rates and assumptions are not guaranteed and may be subject to change. As in all assumptions and examples, individual results may vary based on a wide range of factors unique to each person's situation. All data provided in this book are to be used for informational purposes only. Any slights against individuals, companies, or organizations are unintentional.

DEDICATION

*For my wife, Lori Beth, who is my love
and the Foundation of our family.
To my children who give me life.
To the difficult times in life that have taught
me perseverance and strength, and to all the
people who have given me the opportunity
to make a positive impact in their lives
through the years...
I thank you all.*

Table of Contents

Table of Contents

Wealth Compounded

Strategies for a Secure, Consistent,
and Predicable Retirement Lifestyle...
No Matter What the Stock Market Does

FOREWORD

Hi. I'm Josh Mellberg. I've been in the financial services industry since graduating from college in 2002. During my 18-year career, I've been fortunate enough to have been featured on CNBC, PBS, and Yahoo! Finance. I've also been a regular contributor to the New York Daily News. I learned early on in my career that a successful company must find products that clients need. Throughout my career, my goal has been to teach as many people as possible about the importance of retirement planning and minimizing taxes. I also seek to partner with like-minded and conscientious professionals such as Joshua Schlinsky, the author of this book.

I met Joshua Schlinsky some time ago and immediately learned that we share more than just the same first name. We both started our careers in the financial services industry in the early 2000s and have a passion for helping people prepare for their retirement with sound planning and secure investment strategies. In addition to being an author, Joshua has appeared on "NBC Nightly News" and has been quoted in the *Wall Street Journal*. We also both started our own financial services firms – Joshua owns his own financial service firm, Safe Secure Financial Inc. It's fair to say we've had similar journeys and that we share a passion for helping our clients prepare for their financial future.

Joshua and I also share a passion for helping people navigate the complicated process of planning for retirement. Joshua has had a long successful career and he's committed to meeting the retirement needs of his clients. Whether you're planning for your retirement or providing financial services to your own client, you will find this book informative and useful. Joshua understands the retirement planning process as good as anyone – you've made a great choice!

"The Success of what you are currently doing is based upon the Foundation which immediately precedes it."

Chapter One:

Why I Am Not Ashamed to Die...

It was February 21st, about 11:30 in the morning. My sister, Debbie, had just flown in from New York to see me. As she walked up to my bedside in the hospital she started to cry.

She said, "I've been crying all morning. I didn't know what to expect. I was afraid you would look much worse."

I don't recall what else she said, but *that* I remember. The night before, at 9:35 p.m., just as I had arrived home from a Financial seminar I had given, I suffered a brain hemorrhage. My wife, Lori Beth, rushed me to the hospital and contacted our family.

Although my condition was serious, by the next morning I felt reassured I was going to make it. I was not going to leave this world that day, but the night before, that had been something that was clearly in doubt.

I hadn't slept the entire night. My eyes were wide open, my blood rushed throughout my body, and my mind was racing. I was able to speak, but I wasn't able to converse much.

After standing by my bedside for a while, Debbie sat down in a chair next to Lori Beth and they started talking.

I was just lying in the ICU hospital bed silently when all of the sudden I blurted out, "I would not have been ashamed to die last night!"

Neither Debbie nor Lori Beth had any idea what I meant, or where that came from. My wife later told me she thought I was delirious, but I assured her I was not! As a matter of fact, that may have been the finest moment of clarity I have ever had in my entire life.

The Finest Moment of Clarity

You see, four years earlier I was researching something for a client and I came across the Antioch College website. At the top left of the page was a quote from educator and U.S. Congressman Horace Mann. It read:

"Be ashamed to die before you have won some victory for humanity."

I was so struck by that quote, I vividly remember reading it over and over.

"Be ashamed to die before you have won some victory for humanity."

That quote went to my very core.

At that time, I had only been in the financial business for about two years. I was still finding my way, but I felt as though I was missing something in my life. I did not feel like I was making the positive difference in people's lives as I had in my previous career.

My Past Life as a Funeral Director

Prior to coming into the Financial field in 2001, I had been a funeral director my entire professional life. Yes, a funeral director. Up until the ripe old age of 41.

That was a job of purpose. A job where I came home from work every night knowing that I had made a positive difference in people's lives. My desire and my need to have that positive impact in other people's lives is something that had been instilled in me from my youth. My father was a rabbi of a congregation, and my mother, a teacher. I have always known, from a young age, that I would do something to serve our community and make a positive impact in people's lives, just as each of my parents did in their lives.

The night I had my hemorrhagic stroke, I literally didn't know if I would make it through the night. My mind was awash with thought.

I thought about my wife Lori, who I love so dearly. I have always wanted to protect her and provide for her.

My children are my life. Without them I am nothing. All night I thought...

They may lose their dad even younger than I lost mine.

The absolute clarity of "life" was virtually indescribable in that moment. I am certain that a few of you who are reading this have faced such a moment in your life. You cannot help but reflect on the life you have and the life you have lived up until that moment.

So, as Debbie and Lori Beth sat a few feet from my bed, in those uncomfortable vinyl chairs, I just blurted out, "I would not have been ashamed to die last night."

Victories for Humanity

No, at that moment I would not have been ashamed to die because I knew I had won many victories for humanity. I spent more than 20 years as a funeral director! I had spent many years being there for people and helping them through one of the most difficult times of their lives.

At that time, however, I wasn't sure I was doing the same in the financial field. There wasn't daily positive feedback. I was no longer hearing, "Thank you so much for helping us through this difficult time."

Was I still making a difference in people's lives?

A Particular Insight

As time has moved on, I have learned I am making a difference ... which is why I continue to do so.

You see, my experience as a funeral director gave me a particular insight not everyone has...

Insight into people's lives.

My past experience gives me a unique perspective to recognize what's truly important to my clients; family, children . . . the importance of being able to reflect and feel good about what they've done. The importance of peace of mind and the ability to enjoy their lives and lifestyles in later years.

Because isn't that what it's all about?

Over the years, as I made the arrangements so many people would tell me, "I am so grateful we had these years together. Grateful we had the money and ability to enjoy these years."

I had been told by so many wives, "I am so grateful that we had a good life and my husband has seen to it that I won't have to worry about money now that he is gone."

But I was also told by many that it had been difficult. Although they had worked hard their whole lives, they had not saved enough money or had lost much of what they had to the financial markets or bad business investments.

It took some time in the financial business for me to realize that I can have a similar positive impact on people's lives by helping them to have money and security in their retirement so they can enjoy their lives. So they can be with their families, travel, and spoil their grandchildren, just as Lori Beth and I are spoiling our two grandchildren. (Hopefully more on the way soon!)

My family is my driving force and I want to enjoy them without financial anxiety weighing me down. This is something I try to help each and every family I meet with to achieve. Perhaps writing this book will help those who go through these pages begin to gather a foundation of knowledge regarding safe and secure financial planning. With the right strategy, you can create the stability and peace of mind to live the retirement lifestyle you have worked so hard to achieve.

But Where Is the Market When You Need It?

I find it unfortunate, but many people have been conditioned by Wall Street and money managers to keep ALL their money at risk in the market.

"The market always comes back."

This is something that everyone who pushes the market will say, and to a certain extent they're correct. But that doesn't mean you "win". The point isn't that the market comes back, it's "Where is the market when you need it?"

Many people were very close to retirement in 2007. When the 2008 crash happened, I can't tell you how many had to change those plans. Some lost 30%, 40%, even 50% of their savings and had to postpone retirement...and many who were already in retirement were forced to change their lifestyle.

Countless people have told me similar stories . . . I'm sure you have a friend (or two) who suffered a similar fate.

It's a Powerful Marketing Machine

In his book *The Compound Effect*, Darren Hardy wrote that we have been subconsciously conditioned by the continuous onslaught of the media in so many ways that we have been unable to break free from that conditioning.

Wall Street has a powerful marketing machine. We have been conditioned to keep all our money at risk in the market and to believe that "the market always comes back."

But we don't understand how long that can take and how devastating those losses can be in the meantime. Until it comes back, we don't fully understand how our lives can be derailed.

Don't worry, the market *will* always come back. If you are 35 years old, perhaps it's not a big concern.

But most of you reading this are likely age 50 or above. (Kudos to those of you who are younger and reading this. You are never too young to start your Financial knowledge and planning.)

For those of you over age 50, let me ask you this: Do you always need more money? Is it worth the risk? Or does it make more sense to have the safety and security that can ensure you have the money that you need?

I can tell you from my life's experiences, and the thousands of people I met while I was a funeral director, that the most important thing people conveyed to me was how *grateful* they were for the peace of mind they had in their retirement by having the financial stability and income they needed to enjoy their lives.

If I can help to bring that to the people I work with, then I know I am continuing to make a positive difference in people's lives.

The Right Foundation

Toward the end of my first year in the financial business, I attended a financial planning conference in San Diego. During that conference, the main speaker started with the following quote:

> *"The success of what you are currently doing is based upon the foundation which immediately precedes it."*
>
> **- Unknown**

Not only did he start with that quote, but he repeated it continuously over the next two days. So much so that it brought a chuckle to the crowd when we knew it was coming.

"The success of what you are doing is based upon the foundation which immediately precedes it."

That quote stuck with me . . . and he had repeated it over and over for a reason. With each step we take, we set a foundation for the next step. By doing so, we create a solid base to move forward on in life.

This quote means so much to me.

When I got home, I had each of my sons write that quote down and repeat it daily.

To this day, my children will call me and recite the quote. Yes, we even get a chuckle out of it.

As I write this book, my youngest son (who is in his mid-twenties) just finished his second year running his own business, a business he started from scratch.

When we spoke the other day, we went over his numbers. I expressed to him how proud I am of him, to see how well he has done.

He said to me, "Thanks, Dad . . . 'The success of what you are currently doing is based upon the foundation which immediately precedes it!' Thanks to that advice, next year will be even better."

As parents, we want our children to be successful as they grow. To do that, we provide them with a foundation of love, stability, education, and, for many, faith. These foundational tools help our children become successful in life.

In my financial practice, I want to provide my clients with a foundation of education so that they will be able to make the wisest decision that is best for them.

Let's start with that foundation!

Chapter Two:

The Gathering Storm Facing America

What I am about to tell you will likely not come as a shock, but it still needs to be said... The world is changing!

If you don't believe me, just look at our national debt and the economies of all the nations around the world. It is a tenuous time filled with unprecedented problems. There is general insecurity about what the future will bring.

Some financial gurus don't believe storms are gathering. They keep shouting, "Everything is okay in America." Until recently, the proud residents of Puerto Rico had survived many storms. Some probably thought two major hurricanes crossing right over Puerto Rico would never happen.

Sadly, it did.

Two storms gathered off their shores and unfortunately took the same path, wreaking major havoc across the beautiful island of Puerto Rico. As of the writing of this book, most of the island is without power and residents are living day by day.

One of the gathering storms we face is the ballooning national debt. In an article published on April 25, 2016, Scott Brown from Raymond James suggests the government's 20 **trillion**-dollar debt is not a problem.

He agrees, "Yes, the deficit is large," but then also says, "No, it's not a problem."

Really? I think most Americans feel it's not only a problem, but a gathering storm ready to cause damage to America.

Let's dig into why Brown thinks differently.

He first suggests the recent rise in the national debt is a normal response to the latest recession, similar to what happened during the Great Depression. "Revenues fell. Recession–related spending rose. As the economy recovered, recession-related spending went away, and tax receipts improved. The debt is now down to 2.5% of GDP, which is sustainable."

Sustainable? That scares me. It might scare you too. I want a financial fortress if something goes bad, not a plan that is barely sustainable . . . barely staying ahead of the next market downturn.

Brown also quips, "People are concerned about the long-term amassed debt (then a gnarly 19 trillion number)."

(The debt is even more as of the writing on this book: Over 20 million and growing. In fact, in March of 2018, President Trump signed a $1 trillion-dollar Omnibus bill, making it even bigger.[1])

Here is my favorite quote from the above-referenced article:

"There is no magic level of debt that gets an economy in trouble."

Why? Well, because Brown believes the government can, and does, print money to solve the problem. The scary belief is that America will literally print money to repay the debt and still keep its high rating.

Here is the problem (and what may cause the gathering storm): If we have another recession, or a significant downturn in the economy, America might not be able to keep kicking the "debt can" down the road. An individual can only borrow so much money or acquire so much debt before a day of reckoning must happen.

The same principle applies to America's debt. You may think a country can keep printing money without any long-term effects . . . but that's not the case. Printing money may help in the short term and could perhaps work long term; yet, in most cases, if you keep acquiring more debt, at some point you have to pay the piper. If that were to happen, it could be like a hurricane striking at the financial heart of this amazing country.

Regardless, it is important to know the steps you can take to protect yourself from these gathering storms.

Will You Live Longer Than You Expect?

Many Americans are insecure about their financial futures...

"Will I have enough money to live off of?"

"Am I saving enough?"

"Will I still be able to afford this house/car/lifestyle?"

When it comes to retirement, for most Americans, the answer is a sad, resounding "No."

Why is this the case?

People are living longer and, believe it or not, many of us are outliving our retirement. Not only are we spending *more* in retirement, we also have market volatility to deal with. The 4% withdrawal rule is a thing of the past and more and more Americans fail simply because they procrastinate. They put off financial planning until it's too late.

Running Out of Income

Most of the people I talk to are concerned about outliving their money.

"I don't want to outlive my money."

"I want to make sure my money is here as long as I am."

I hate to say it, but for a lot of us, the possibility of outliving our money is a very real possibility.

Do you know someone in their 90s? I do. I know several. Thanks to modern medicine and the pharmaceutical industry, people are living longer these days. For those of us who are a bit jaded, think profits! There is a great deal of money to be made by the medical and pharmaceutical companies to keep us living longer.

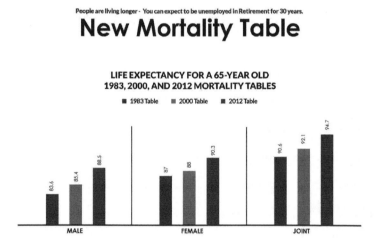

Image courtesy of Wealth Education Group

The problem is that most of us haven't planned for this increased life expectancy. Most of our portfolios weren't designed to last that long.

The Financial Rules of Yesteryear Are No Longer Valid

Not only are people living longer, they're spending more.

How much money do you think you need in retirement? Do you think you will need more or less?

For a long time, the financial rule, so to speak, has been that most of us will only need 75% of our income in retirement. But for the first 15 years of retirement, I have found that my clients need *more* income!

It seems counterintuitive, but let me ask you this...

When you go on vacation, do you spend more or less than you do when you're working?

Of course, you spend more money on vacation! You have more time on your hands!

Retirement is a lot like vacation. When you're busy working, not only are you earning money, you're spending less. Retirement is kind of like an extended vacation. Most of us tend to spend *more* money in retirement!

Now, I'm not saying that it's impossible to live off the same income, but to suggest living on anything less isn't reasonable or responsible.

A Story of a Lovely Lady

Let me tell you a story about a lovely lady I know, my mom!

Mom recently turned 85 years old. When I was a teenager my parents divorced. As a single mom she needed to earn more money so she left her career as a teacher for a corporate job.

My mother is originally from Scranton, Pennsylvania. My grandparents had emigrated from Eastern Europe, and all five of their kids were born and raised in Scranton. Mom was the second of five. She told me stories of her father waiting to eat dinner until all the children had eaten so he could be sure there was enough food for them. Money was scarce.

This is something that has stayed with my mom her whole life. Once she was divorced and living on her own, she worked tirelessly, rarely spent a nickel, and saved everything.

When she turned 65, I realized it was time for mom to retire. She had saved well and was lucky enough to have a small pension from her job. With that, plus Social Security, I knew she would be OK.

So, I went to see her and said, "Mommy, it's time for you to retire. It's time to get a new apartment closer to me and your grandkids, and start living your life."

Well, you might have thought I was coming from another planet with that idea. Mom was so laser focused on working and saving, she hadn't even thought of retiring.

"I will have to think about it and call your sisters to see what they think."

Well I knew she would say that, so I had already called my sisters, both of whom live far from South Florida, and told them: "When mommy calls you about this, back me up, it's time for her to retire and enjoy her life."

Indeed, mom called my sisters and they reinforced my suggestion, or shall we say, my mandate! The company mom worked for threw her a wonderful, well-deserved retirement party to which my wife Lori Beth and I were invited. I helped her buy a new condo much closer to where we lived, a new car, and told her to start traveling.

My sisters each have children for her to visit in New York and Israel, so mom started to take trips. In addition to visiting her grandchildren, she was able to get together with her siblings and vacation in several National Parks. She even took a cruise to Alaska.

Mom spent a lot of money early on in her retirement years. All that travel wasn't cheap!

When Mom retired in 1998, the market was doing well. She was two years into enjoying her retirement when the 2000 to 2003 market crash came. For many it was devastating, but my mom didn't have any financial worries because her money was safely protected.

In 2008, when most retirees and pre-retirees were losing 30% to 50% of their hard-earned money, again mom didn't have to worry one bit. Her money had grown and was protected. Market volatility did not impact my mom's lifestyle, not one bit!

When mom was about 78, I picked her up from the airport. She was coming back from visiting one of my sisters and her grandchildren.

"How was your trip, mom?"

Her reply caught me off guard.

"I'm not going to go again."

Immediately I started thinking...*Uh oh, she must have gotten into an argument with my sister.* (After all, my family is no different than most!)

But mom said, "No, I'm just getting older. The arthritis in my knees has gotten worse and it makes traveling difficult. I have really enjoyed these last twelve years. I had traveled more than I ever thought I would. I have spent quality time with my siblings and grandchildren, but now I am content to stay at home with my boyfriend and take it easy."

At first, I felt bad that mom didn't feel she could travel anymore, but then I felt a deep sense of pride. I had helped her make the decision to retire and to enjoy her life, which she had worked so hard for. She deserved it and earned it!

Mom spent a lot of money in those first twelve years of retirement enjoying her life and doing what she wanted to do . . . but since then she hasn't spent much at all.

Many times, I've heard my clients say they expect to spend less money on their lifestyles in retirement, but I don't necessarily find this to be true. This is not just a reality I have learned from my own mother, but over the years I have heard similar stories from clients of mine and parents of my clients. In the early years of your retirement, you should expect to spend more, not less.

Tornadoes vs. Hurricanes

What is the difference between a tornado and a hurricane?

A tornado is unexpected. It could be a beautiful day . . . but within a few minutes, a storm rolls in and suddenly a tornado is on top of you!

A hurricane is different, right? It's expected.

(As a native of South Florida, I have firsthand knowledge of hurricanes.)

We can track it thousands of miles out at sea. We know how wide the eye is and how fast the winds are. We also have a pretty good idea of where it's going. We even give it a name!

Everyone has seen a meteorologist on TV, standing in the pouring rain, braving 80mph winds, screaming, "IN JUST FIVE HOURS, THE EYE OF THE HURRICANE IS GOING TO PASS DIRECTLY OVER US!" (I think those people are crazy!)

Hurricanes are predictable, but of course, the day after the storm passes, you see footage of all the people being rescued from their roofs wrapped in Red Cross blankets. People who either couldn't escape due to lack of knowledge or resources, or made the decision to "ride it out."

Tornadoes are unpredictable, but hurricanes we can see coming . . . and I feel the same way about the stock market right now.

I'm going to give you three FACTS about the current market:

1. March 2018 marked the 9-year anniversary of the current bull market. From February 2009 to February 2018, the S&P 500 has averaged a 14.4% annual return.

Have you come to accept this as "how it should be" and become complacent?

2. The Schiller PE ratio right now is at 29. For those of you not familiar with that, it's the cyclical price to earnings ratio (P/E ratio) for the S&P 500. Historically, that ratio has been closer to 16. Again, right now it's at 32.89.

Let me put that into perspective. *Over the past 147 years, we have only seen P/E ratios this high THREE times: 1929, 2000, and today.*

3. Lastly, our 10-year treasury interest rates are around 2.4%. Over the same 147-year history, we have experienced rates this low 16 times.

This interest rate isn't unprecedented, but we've never had both low interest rates and high stock valuations happen at the same time. Every other time in history, one of those factors balanced out the other. That's what's unprecedented.

So, what does that mean for us?

I'm not saying that we've reached the peak of this market. No one knows that.

And I'm also not saying that you should take all your money and move it to cash. That's probably unwise.

What I am saying is that now is the time to gain perspective and take control of your future. It's about taking a deep breath, looking at your situation today, and making a plan you can depend on . . . regardless of any tornadoes or hurricanes that might be coming.

You need a plan that walks you into the future with confidence.

Market Volatility

"The line separating investment and speculation, which is never bright and clear, becomes blurred still further when most market participants have recently enjoyed triumphs. Nothing sedates rationality like large doses of effortless money. After a heady experience of that kind, normally sensible people drift into behavior akin to that of Cinderella at the ball. They know that overstaying the festivities — that is, continuing to speculate in companies that have gigantic valuations relative to the cash they are likely to generate in the future — will eventually bring on pumpkins and mice. But they nevertheless hate to miss a single minute of what is one helluva party. Therefore, the giddy participants all plan to leave just seconds before midnight. There's a problem, though: They are dancing in a room in which the clocks have no hands."

Warren Buffett[2]

In 2007, I met a typical couple. George was 64 and Marsha was 63. He had spent the last 25 years working for the same company, had a saved well in his 401(k), and was planning on retiring the following year.

The couple came to meet with me twice, and each time we spoke about a comprehensive plan with a foundation of Safe & Secure strategies. But, as happened with others as well back then, they decided not to implement those strategies. *The Market always wins*, they must have thought.

Fast forward to about six months following the 2008 market crash, I answered the phone and heard...

"Hi, Joshua."

She reminded me who she was. It was Marsha.

"Do you remember me?"

"Yes, of course. How are you?"

She paused and through the phone, I could hear her take a long breath.

"I'm not doing well, truth be told. Neither is George. While we were in the mall the other day, he got a call from his money manager. I watched as his face turned sheet white."

"Oh, no," I said genuinely distraught. I knew where this was headed.

"He lost 45% of his portfolio. There's no way we can retire now." She was on the verge of tears. "Can we come and see you?"

We'll go into this topic in more depth later, but when it comes to retirement, most Americans lose money because of market volatility.

Think about the last 17 years. In the early 2000s, we had three years of market downturns and in 2008, we had another two years of losses. From 2000 to 2009, there was a -6.9% ROR in the market.[3]

By the time people recovered their losses from 2000-2002, they lost it all again in 2008 and 2009. It's 2018 and people are just now getting back to where they were before market crashed in 2000. Think about all those people who were supposed to retire. Because of market volatility, they had to postpone their retirement.

The 4% Rule

Market volatility has also affected our distribution rates.

Most of us only have enough saved to live off. Most of us aren't independently wealthy or can sustain a 30% loss of our assets in retirement. Most of us are concerned we may run out of money in retirement.

So, how do we plan accordingly?

Let's say you need $4,000 a month in retirement. Social Security could provide you with $2,000 a month and you have X in assets. How do you come up with the balance? How are you going to make sure that your X in assets is going to cover the difference for the rest of your life?

"The 4% Rule" was created in 1994 by financial advisor, William Bengen. Prior to the 1990s, 5% was considered a safe amount when it came to annual retirement withdrawals. Bengen was unconvinced that 5% was enough, so he studied the market from 1926 to 1976, a 50-year period. He paid particularly close attention to the 1930s and early 1970s, periods when the market experienced heavy downturns.

His conclusion? That even during historically volatile periods, a portfolio could *probably* survive for 33-years at a 4% withdrawal rate.[4]

The Morningstar Report

In 2013, a new academic report was published by Morningstar, an investment research and management firm. Due to the market volatility of the early and late 2000s, the 4% rule has changed to the 2.8% rule.[2] Meaning, if you have $1 million in your retirement fund and want it to *probably* last 30-plus years, you are advised to only withdraw $28,000 annually.

Is that enough?

Personally, I can tell you, that isn't enough. It isn't enough for my family, my friends, or my clients.

And it doesn't get any better.

According to Morningstar, when you combine the new mortality rates with a 2.8% withdrawal rate, most Americans need to save 42.9% *more* for retirement. That's staggering.

It's Simply Human Nature

Based on all this, most of us should start saving more money immediately . . . right?

But the problem is, most of us procrastinate. Life is busy and gets in the way of many of the things we know we should do.

The $100 Million Dollar Man

Over the last few months I met an individual worth millions and millions of dollars. He is a man of significant wealth and knows he needs an estate plan. He knows that if something happens to him before he has a chance to create an estate plan, the government will seize a significant percentage of his assets. Assets he has built over the course of his life. He told me he wants to ensure his family and the charities that are important to him are well taken care of after he passes, but he has re-scheduled our meeting several times.

When we spoke the other day, I simply said, "You have been telling me you want to meet and have a plan to protect your estate from excessive taxation, yet you keep putting it off. Why?"

His reply to me was insightful, truthful, and thought-provoking. He said,

"You know, Josh, the easiest thing to procrastinate is something that's not knocking at your door."

Wow, it really struck me when he said that. It is so true.

Most people don't see long-term financial planning as an immediate need. Most people procrastinate.

But I can assure you, without question, that money issues will *always* come knocking. The need for Strategic Safe & Secure financial planning, not to mention Tax mitigation planning, will rear its ugly head.

Unfortunately for most, this need tends to arise at the most inopportune time. Typically, the need arises after a market downturn, *after* a significant amount of money has already been lost. Because most of us tend to procrastinate, we end up being more reactive than proactive.

"Why didn't I do something about this earlier?"

Will a Market Crash Come Knocking at Your Door?

Procrastination is human nature . . . but people who are proactive tend to be more successful. Wouldn't you agree?

Everyone should be able to live (and continue living) without worry or concern. We all deserve peace of mind. And people should be able to have the lifestyle they have worked so hard for in retirement.

Could taking action now help you find more peace of mind or give you a better lifestyle? It might. That is why hundreds of people have chosen to work with me on a more personal level.

We design a financial plan that is best suited for their individual needs. If we both sit down at some point, I will follow the same process with you. I would assess your situation and tailor a plan specific to your needs.

The way my firm engineers financial strategies is no different than the way a car manufacturer designs and builds new cars. A race car is built for speed, whereas an 18-wheeler is built for heavy lifting.

We can engineer your financial plan to achieve maximum efficiency for your personal situation, your goals, and what's important to you.

Safe and Secure Planning

Before we go any further, I must explicitly state that I believe in a foundation of *Safe and Secure financial planning*. In my professional opinion, there is no reason to take on risk when we can get what we want safely and securely.

Look at the current state of the market, for example. March 9, 2009 was the lowest point of the 2008 market crash . . . yet here we are, on a 9-year market run.

Historically, we know this is unsustainable . . . but people are greedy. I'm not being condescending, but we as human beings have a built-in greed factor, we always want just a bit more, and hey, I'm no different. It's human nature.

"Maybe it'll go a little bit higher."

I advise my clients to be logical and prudent. I advise them to take some of their winnings off the table . . . before the market turns and they lose everything.

Clear the Clutter

I want to help you "clear the clutter" and bring focus to your financial life. I'm going to help you create a solid financial foundation so that you can be assured to achieve your financial goals regardless of the market.

Most of us are confused when it comes to finances, and that's really no surprise. We are surrounded by clutter. Financial propaganda is everywhere. For some, this book may even fall into that category...

But I really don't see it that way. My goal is to give you the simple and clear information to resolve any confusion, and that is one of the main reasons for writing this book. Everyone has their biases in this world. One doctor's bias may be to operate, while another doctor may have a bias toward medication and therapy. Your accountant's bias is to save you money on taxes this year. A money manager's bias is to keep all your money in the market.

Here is my bias: I want to protect your money. I want you to have a foundation of safe and secure strategies specific to your individual needs, so you can *Compound your Wealth* even with all the gathering storms happening in America.

Now let's discover three major dates you need to be aware of in the next chapter...

Three Crucial Dates that Changed the Future of the American Retirement System Forever

There are three dates that changed the face and future of the American retirement system. Despite what you may think, this isn't a political argument.

Because of what occurred on those dates, it doesn't matter which candidate you voted for or which political party is in control. The reality is that what occurred on these three dates changed the face and future of the American retirement system, forever. Their impact on the future, cannot be changed by politicians. They are mathematical, empirical facts.

These three dates changed America's retirement system.

January 1, 2008

On **January 1, 2008,** the first baby boomer turned 62 years old and qualified to take early Social Security distributions.

Now, if we were talking about just one baby boomer, that would be fine, but we're not. In fact, every day since, an average of *10,000* (yes, you read that right!) baby boomers turn 62. Every day, 10,000 baby boomers qualify for early Social Security distributions.

January 1, 2011

The second date that changed the American retirement system was **January 1, 2011.**

If you're quick at math you've already figured out why this date matters; January 1, 2011 is when the first baby boomer turned 65 . . . meaning he or she now qualifies for full Social Security benefits.

To top it all off, if he or she is retired and wasn't working at a company that offered health insurance, our baby boomer also gets a new primary healthcare provider . . . Medicare.

And guess what?

Every day since January 1, 2011, we've had a daily average of 10,000 baby boomers turning 65 and qualifying for those same benefits.

Can you imagine potentially 10,000 new Social Security and Medicare recipients every single day?

Never have we seen such a large, seemingly unending stream of people *ready to tap into retirement and healthcare programs <u>at the same time</u>.*

US GOVERNMENT DEPT TO GDP

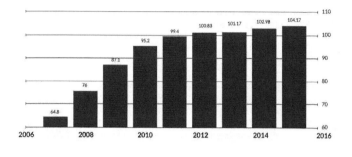

SOURCE: TRADINGECONOMICS.COM | U.S. BUREAU OF PUBLIC DEBT

Where do You Think Taxes are Going?

How do those two dates affect our country?

Take a moment to review the chart above. As you can see, our national debt is trending upward. We'll go into this in more detail later in the book, but based on these current levels...

Where do you think taxes are headed? Do you think they will go down, remain the same, or go up?

I can clearly state that I believe taxes are going up — way up — over the long term. Many of my clients (and most of the people I speak to) agree that taxes must go up. We could potentially see lower rates for a while (which makes smart tax planning *now* even more beneficial), but ultimately these debts must be paid. That means taxes are going to rise.

I strongly believe that traditional planning is failing because most Americans aren't willing to acknowledge and accept this fact.

Yes, this is my belief . . . but it is supported by facts. Mathematical, indisputable facts.

Look again at the chart above. Notice the comparatively small numbers in 2006 and 2007 and then the noticeable spike in 2008.

What does it all mean? The chart above gives us a clue. It represents the percentage of the US government debt in relation to the entire gross domestic product (GDP) of our country. Basically, this graph shows us how much money the government intends to spend (debt) versus how much they anticipate they will earn (by selling U.S. products).

In 2008, the first baby boomers had the opportunity to take Social Security payments. Well . . . some of them did, and it spiked our ratio of debt to the GDP. That's what you see reflected in that graph. The next year, even more eligible baby boomers signed up to receive their promised benefit. Of course, by 2010, there were even more.

In 2011, a steady upward curve begins to appear because, just like health insurance, costs go up a little bit more over time.

How do you think we're going to pay all that money back? This pattern clearly indicates that taxes must be adjusted over the long haul.

Taxes & the Pressure on Cash Flow

Where do you think we are today in relation to historical marginal tax rates? Let's take a look from 1913 to 2018. You can plainly see that taxes have been much higher than they are now.

Top US Federal Tax Bracket History

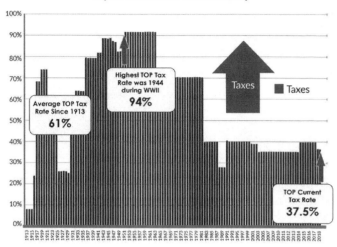

We will show you why this is important.

One of the things that always comes up when I'm meeting with a client is my thoughts on the market. There was a time when I felt that inflation would make the market go up because things just naturally get more expensive over time.

But today, I think that there's a different and more likely scenario. I now think the market is under significant cash-flow pressure, and that cash-flow pressure is going to worsen over time. The third important date will help you understand why...

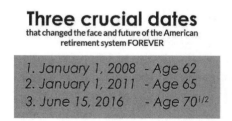

Three crucial dates
that changed the face and future of the American
retirement system FOREVER

1. January 1, 2008 - Age 62
2. January 1, 2011 - Age 65
3. June 15, 2016 - Age 70¹/²

June 15, 2016

Remember those three dates we talked about? We've already talked about 2008 and 2011.

Now let's talk about the third date: **June 15, 2016.**

What happened on that date? The very first baby boomer hit age 70.5 and was required to begin taking minimum distributions (RMDs) from certain retirement plans, including the traditional IRA and 401k plans.

Now, let's talk about why that matters.

When you have a tax-deferred retirement account, like a traditional IRA, you avoid paying taxes on the contributions you make.

You've also grown your money without taxation.

Think back on the storm argument I made in the previous chapter. Hurricanes are predictable whereas tornadoes are not.

If market volatility is like a hurricane, then taxes are like a tornado. We have no idea when taxes are going to hit because we have absolutely no control over them.

Think about it. We can move our money out of the market at any time, but the *government* controls when to increase (and decrease) our taxes.

Back to your tax-deferred retirement account. The government has allowed you to grow your money tax-free, but the IRS doesn't let that go on forever, so at age 70.5 they require participants to begin taking taxable distributions, otherwise known as RMDs. RMDs are based on age, life expectancy, and the previous year's balance.

Age	Withdrawal Percentage	Age	Withdrawal Percentage	Age	Withdrawal Percentage
70	3.650%	82	5.848%	94	10.989%
71	3.774%	83	6.135%	95	11.628%
72	3.906%	84	6.452%	96	12.346%
73	4.049%	85	6.757%	97	13.158%
74	4.202%	86	7.092%	98	14.085%
75	4.367%	87	7.463%	99	14.925%
76	4.545%	88	7.874%	100	15.873%
77	4.717%	89	8.333%	101	16.949%
78	4.926%	90	8.772%	102	18.182%
79	5.128%	91	9.259%	103	19.231%
80	5.348%	92	9.804%	104	20.408%
81	5.587%	93	10.417%	105	22.222%

Take a look at the chart above.

Currently, the government dictates that you take your account balance from December 31 of the prior year and divide it by the number in the Distribution Period column next to your age. They call it a uniform table because that's what everybody uses even if you aren't married, widowed, or married to an older spouse.

Sound complicated?

You may ask, *how does the government come up with this stuff?!* Well, that I can't tell you, but let's look at an example to make it easier to understand.

Sally, a retiree who is 70.5 years old, has $100,000 in her IRA. She must start taking minimum distributions, so according to the **RMD chart above,** she must take the balance of her IRA and divide it by 27.4%. That means that her distribution now is $3,649 per year.

Let's reverse this and consider what percentage of her overall balance that distribution is. In this case, the required distribution of $3,649 divided by $100,000 is 3.649%.

(That percentage will continue to go up . . . read on.)

Well that doesn't sound so bad, right? It's less than 4%, which is what many traditional retirement planners suggest for withdrawals. Maybe the IRS is onto something with their formula!

Or . . . maybe not.

Because in a moment, you're going to find out that 3.659% is a very large, completely unsustainable distribution rate in today's low-yield environment.

Low Bond Yields and Safe Portfolio Withdrawal Rates

Like I mentioned earlier, Morningstar is a leading investment research firm. Many of you have probably heard of them. They provide accurate, insightful, unbiased reports that are used by countless brokerage firms, planners, asset management firms, and other finance professionals.

In 2013, they published a study of their findings on low yields and safe withdrawal rates from retirement plans[6]. The authors of the study were notable and accomplished PhD's with advanced degrees in economics and finance. They concluded that our ability to avoid running out of money in retirement was based on taking no more than 2.8% a year from our accounts.

Now take a moment and just think about that. "2.8%." On a $100,000 account for our retiree, Sally, that would be $2,800...

That's quite a difference from the $3,649 the IRS is requiring (RMD) Sally to take. In fact, if the goal is to be highly certain you won't run out of money in retirement, it's over 30% more than what Morningstar's experts consider "safe".

Morningstar's study defines your probability of success based on your account not going to zero. In other words, it defines success as your ability to climb back down the mountain after scaling the top. Success, in this report, does not mean that your basis (the principal, invested capital) in your account is preserved but that your account will not run down to a $0 balance before you die.

I don't know about you, but that wouldn't make me feel too good. Would that breed confidence for you?

<u>In this academic paper written by Morningstar experts in economics and finance, that is the definition of success.</u> They don't define success as mass accumulation of funds, they define it as your ability to maintain a balance greater than zero in your account, despite taking annual distributions at various rates.

When you think about it...

If the required minimum distribution rate in year one for a healthy, vigorous 70.5-year-old is roughly 3.649%,

And

If we know that percentage will go up every year,

AND

If we consider the stock and bond market as one huge portfolio with roughly 10,000 baby boomers turning 70.5 years old each day,

We start to see that this is creating a tremendous amount of cash-flow pressure. That pressure is building . . . and it's only going to get worse.

By age 80, the divisor for the minimum distribution goes down (from 27.4% at 70.5, to 18.7% at age 80). This means that the required amount of distributions from your IRA and 401k account goes up.

Let's see what that does to our RMD.

Consider that you are now 80 years old. If we take that same $100,000 and we do that division, that means the RMD now is $5,347 or 5.35% as a distribution rate.

That's almost *twice* as much as Morningstar advises to avoid hitting a $0 balance.

I believe that's an unsustainable amount of pressure on the market as approximately 10,000 new retirees turn 70.5 years old every day and another 10,000 or so turn 80. Still, you might think that's going to slow down eventually. There aren't going to be ten thousand boomers turning 65 years old every day forever.

While that's true, with advancements in medical technology, more and more retirees are living healthy and productive lives. My mother is 85, and thank God, as of today, is in very good health. And there are more people living past age 100 than ever before.

This means we're going to carry the burden of the boomers for a very long time.

Facts of a Changing World

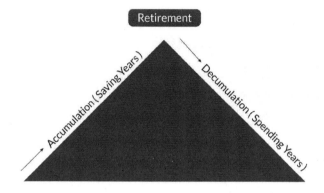

1987: What We Thought Retirement Income Planning Would Be

Retirement

Accumulation (Saving Years)

Decumulation (Spending Years)

The accumulation of assets is different than the decumulation of assets. Planning your descent is more important than the climb.

Mt. Everest

Many financial planners and professionals focus almost all of their attention and efforts on helping you grow or accumulate money for retirement. They may use any number of different investments and strategies to get that pile of money to grow, and in many cases, they're very good at it. Some of you may have worked with one of these advisors over the years, and though you may have experienced a few bumps along the way, your advisor may have done a really good job of helping you grow your nest egg for retirement.

The problem is that many financial professionals specialize exclusively on the accumulation phase which starts around age 20 or 25 and goes through about age 60 to 65. But "accumulation" is only one phase of your financial life. If your current financial advisor is really only helping you <u>on your way</u> to retirement, then they're leaving you exposed to a number of dangers that could affect you <u>through</u> retirement.

Do you know what a Sherpa is?

Sherpas are the most experienced Himalayan guides that accompany those setting out to climb Mt. Everest. Sherpas are considered the best of the best; they have expert knowledge of the terrain making them invaluable to climbers tackling Everest for the first time. These guys know what to expect.

What's interesting is that these Sherpas, or guides, are even more valuable to climbers on their way back down the mountain than they are on the way up.

Why? Because the descent is far more treacherous than the climb. Between 1921 and 2006, of the people who didn't make it back alive (it is a very perilous journey, after all), 56% died on the descent and another 17% died after turning back.[7]

Far more people die on Mt. Everest after they've already reached the summit, after they've reached their "goal" and started coming back down. Either their bodies have trouble acclimating to the oxygen levels or they simply don't have the expertise and endurance to get safely back to camp.

That's why you can't put a price tag on a Sherpa. Their ability to show you the way and help you avoid the crevasses and dangers ahead and to stick to the course that gets you safely back down the mountain is invaluable.

Mountain climbing is a lot like planning for retirement. Many people (including financial professionals) focus on the climb up, figuring out the best ways to invest and accumulate money for the day they hit their summit.

On the other hand, most people spend very little time thinking about the rest of the journey. After years of faithful saving and investing, they have no real plan for how to wisely use their nest egg to ensure it lasts throughout retirement. They have no real plan to make sure they get safely down the mountain.

Most of us need a **Financial Sherpa**. Most of us not only need an accumulation guide, a guide up the mountain, but more importantly in many instances, need a Decumulation guide, a guide to get us safely back down the mountain. Most of us need a Financial Sherpa to ensure that what we've built lasts as long as we'll need it.

2017: **What We Know Retirement Income Planning To Be**

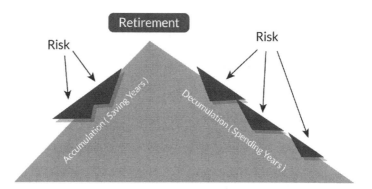

My team of advisors can be your Financial Sherpas. We have expert knowledge of the terrain. We know the dangers ahead and we know the best paths to take. Without an experienced guide, who knows how you will survive throughout retirement!

I can't imagine anyone looking forward to being stranded at the top of the mountain they just worked so hard to climb.

I also can't imagine any retiree working hard to save and preserve money during their working years just so they can pay a lot of it out in taxes just a few years after retirement. Even worse, I can't imagine a retiree suffering from a market downturn and losing 25% to 40% of the money they worked so hard to save, forced to rely primarily on Social Security to get them through.

So, what does this all mean to you?

With the old-world planning of the 80s and 90s, we thought retirement income planning would be straightforward: accumulate money while you work, retire, and earn a decent interest rate without risk.

But today, we now know that it may not be such a smooth path. There are risks both as you save, and as you spend.

- The Risk of Increased Taxation
- The Risk of Low Interest Rates
- The Devastating Risk of Losses in the Market

Someone once told me if you stay on the same path, you will eventually get run over.

<u>The world is changing, and we must change with it.</u>

Chapter Four:

What is Your 401(k) Really Worth?

I magine two business owners. They're partners, but the partnership isn't equal. Partner A owns 75% of the business and Partner B owns 25%.

Retirement Plan 401K/IRA

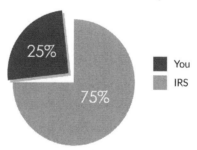

Now imagine that Partner B, the *minority* partner, makes all the rules.

The two partners work together for over 30 years, then one day, Partner B tells Partner A that his share of the business is now 35%.

Retirement Plan 401K/IRA

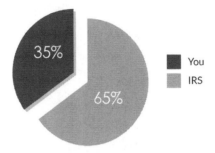

Remember, Partner B makes all the rules. Whatever he or she says, goes. No explanation is needed.

Just like that, Partner A is down 10%.

You would think long and hard before you went into business with a partner who controlled all the shots regarding his or her ownership percentage.

So, why do so many Americans make that exact decision each and every day?

Tax-Deferred Doesn't Mean Tax-Free

Where do you have most of your money? Is it in an IRA or 401(k) like many Americans?

If you're an entrepreneur, have your own business, are a real estate investor, etc., then the likelihood is that most of your money is not in an IRA or 401(k).

But if you're an employee or have your own business with a highly-compensated retirement plan, then the chances are the bulk of your saving is an IRA, 401(k), or other qualified account.

A qualified account typically allows the contributor to deposit pre-tax earnings into the plan. The account growth is also tax-deferred. Taxes are paid later at regular income rates, when funds are taken out.

This sounds like a great deal for most. And it might be for a portion of your money. However, having all your money in a place that is not diversified against the threat of rising future taxes could significantly impact your retirement savings.

Qualified money can be found in a 401(k), IRA, 403(b), 457, etc. It is money that is yet to be taxed. Non-qualified money is money that is stored everywhere else. It has already been taxed.

Most of us keep our money in qualified accounts and deferred (and continue to defer) our taxes.

And why not? For decades, many financial experts have told the American public that using a qualified plan is the best way to plan for retirement.

But tax-deferred doesn't mean tax-free. Throughout my financial career, I have been surprised to learn many people do not realize that. Most Americans don't realize they're going to have to pay those taxes eventually, and pay them at what the tax income rates will be at that time.

The IRS Makes All the Rules

When you chose to defer your taxes, you select the government as a retirement partner.

It may sound like a good idea, but when you partner with the government (the IRS) they become the minority partner.

Most of the money is yours. You're Partner A. But because we have no control over the tax rates, the IRS makes all the rules. When it's time to withdraw your money from a qualified account, you have no idea what the tax rate will be.

Let me put this another way.

You need a loan from the bank. You walk in to your local branch and submit your application.

"Congratulations! You're approved," a friendly bank teller informs you.

"Great! What's my interest rate? What will I have to pay you back?"

The bank teller's smile grows wider. "You know what? Don't worry about that today. We'll figure out that out later. At a future date."

Well . . . would you take that check from the bank without knowing what they're going to charge you?

Image courtesy of Reynolds.[8]

How Will Taxes Affect Your Retirement?

When we partner with the IRS, we are agreeing to a loan without knowing the interest charges. We know what the tax rates are today, but we have no idea what they will be in the future.

When we chose to invest a large portion of our money in a qualified account, we are depositing our money pre-tax. Because we are deferring taxes *now*, it will be taxed *later*, when we need to withdraw it in retirement. This affects social security taxation as well...meaning many of us won't be in a lower tax bracket. It's much more likely we'll be in the same or a higher tax bracket.

Taking the Uncertainty Out of Predicting the Future

Have you heard of Ed Slott? He is a very well-known CPA and published author who believes that taxes are the single biggest retirement risk.

He said:

> *"You may think you will be in a lower tax bracket later, but you don't know.[9]"*

He also said:

> *"A Roth 401(k) or a Roth IRA takes the uncertainty out of predicting the future.[10]*

Depending on your personal situation, taxes could be your biggest risk!

Most Americans aren't aware they will be taxed when it's time to withdraw their money from their qualified accounts. Most Americans haven't planned for that extra cost.

We already know that most of us are saving less and spending more . . . how do you think taxes will affect Americans' retirement plans?

Where are Taxes Headed?

I asked this question earlier in the book, but I want to ask it again...

Where do you think taxes will be in the future? Will they be higher, will they be lower, or will they be the same?

Most people tell me, "I think they're going to be higher."

"Why?" I ask them.

"The debt we're in."

"Someone has to pay for it."

"Social Security and Medicare."

Taxes *will* be higher. Eventually. They may continue to dip for a bit, but they must go up. It's simple mathematics.

It really isn't about politics or who's in office. Yes, those decisions affect the current moment, but our financial life isn't dictated in a moment. It is determined over the course of many, many years.

And over the course of those many, many years, mathematics will be the true gauge of this upcoming taxation spike. There is no escaping the mathematics of where our country is today.

Right now, we're at an all-time low . . . but where taxes go in the future is yet to be seen.

Will Taxes Double?

In 2009, David Walker, a former Controller General of the United States, made a bold statement. He predicted that, based on current fiscal tax revenue and national debt, future taxes will have to double, otherwise our country will go bankrupt.[11]

I don't believe that taxes will double. I don't believe that we're going to go bankrupt . . . but I *do* believe that changes will be made simply because of mathematics. They will have to!

At the end of the day, it doesn't matter which political party is in power at the time. No one is going to take away your Social Security because there would be pitchforks and fire in the streets.

And everybody wants to get re-elected, so, regardless of party, our politicians are going to have to pay for our debt somehow. One of the best ways Congress knows how to do this is . . . to raise taxes. At some point, Congress will probably have to raise taxes, in some form, to help pay for the debt. The question for you is:

> *"Are you going to take the uncertainty out of predicting the future by putting a good portion of your money in tax-free accounts?"*

For some of you, that option is there. Later on, it will be one of the strategies we look into.

Two Systems of Taxation

There are two different ways to look at taxation.

> Louis D. Brandeis was a Supreme Court Justice from 1919 to 1939. The following are some of his thoughts on tax avoidance:
>
> "I lived in Alexandria, Virginia. Near the Supreme Court chambers is a toll bridge across the Potomac. When in a rush, I pay the toll and get home early. However, I usually drive outside the downtown section of the city and cross the Potomac on a free bridge. The bridge was placed outside the downtown Washington, D.C. area to serve a useful social service: getting drivers to drive an extra mile to help alleviate congestion during rush hour.
>
> "If I went over the toll bridge and through the barrier without paying the toll, I would be committing tax evasion. However, if I drive the extra mile outside the city of Washington and take the free bridge, I am using a legitimate, logical and suitable method of tax avoidance, and I am performing a useful social service by doing so.
>
> "For my tax evasion, I should be punished. For my tax avoidance, I should be commended. The tragedy in life is that so few people know that the free bridge even exists."

Most people who are uninformed have most of their money in qualified plans. When they defer taxes, they create a bond for the government. They don't know what taxes they will owe, just that they owe them.

We've already discussed that the government has a huge debt to pay. We can also imagine the rioting that would ensue if taxes doubled.

But taxes *have* to rise . . . meaning money withdrawn from qualified plans will be affected.

Tax Diversification

Regardless of what the future of taxation looks like, tax diversification is key.

Some people think having all their money in a qualified retirement plan is a good strategy; and for many, it is. If it weren't for 401(k)s, a system that withdraws money automatically, a lot of people wouldn't have any savings at all!

But it is my belief that every wise, prudent financial plan should not only have asset allocation, but tax diversification as well.

A percentage of your money should be in qualified accounts *and* non-qualified accounts. *That* is tax diversification. Everyone should have money saved in an account where your money comes out *tax-free.*

Too often, I meet people who have all their savings in tax-deferred qualified plans. Not only do these plans lack liquidity prior to age $59^{1/2}$, too many people don't understand how these dollars will be taxed and how that taxation will affect your overall future *income.* After all, it's not how much money you have in the future, but how much money you have to spend!

The future of taxation is unknown and its effects on your retirement could be devastating.

I really don't know what tomorrow holds . . . do you? Therefore, let's learn how to have a balanced plan to ensure our success.

Chapter Five:

A Low-Interest Rate Environment

I have had more than one client say to me:

> "Josh, I currently have some money in a CD. I'm only getting 1.25%, but I'm sure rates are going to go up. Perhaps I should wait and see."

Once we start to discuss it, they generally understand that waiting is a fool's game.

Why?

Let's say we wait a year, and let's also give the Fed the benefit of a doubt and say rates go up by a whopping 1% (which I do not think they will).

Does that make a difference in your financial life?

On your $1 million, you can make $22,500 in the second year, instead of the $12,500 you were making a year ago.

But if you had placed your money into a Safe and Secure account averaging just 4% (that's on the very low end), you would make $40,000 the first year and $40,000 the second year. That's $80,000 from your $1 million principal.

If you stay in the CD, getting 1.25% now and 2.25% next year, you only receive $35,000. That's $55,000 less than you would make in a Safe and Secure account.

We Are Financing Everything

Before we continue discussing America's retirement planning crisis, I want to spend a minute talking about interest rates.

Historically, interest rates are at an all-time low.

US FED FUNDS RATE

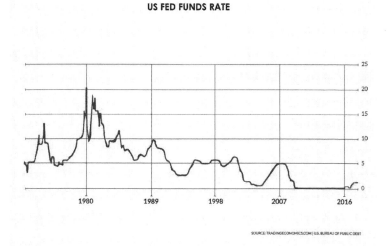

SOURCE: TRADINGECONOMICS.COM | U.S. BUREAU OF PUBLIC DEBT

Many people I speak to think it's a new era, a new low-interest rate environment.

Others think the Fed might raise interest rates a little over time. For interest-bearing accounts, that sounds like a good thing.

"Should I wait to move my money out of my CD because interest rates will go up?"

But if the Fed raises interest rates on interest-bearing accounts, how do you think that will affect our mortgages, car loans, and credit card debt?

Before we make those types of decisions, we really need to understand how interest rates work. In order to create a financial strategy to fit our lifestyle, we really need to be informed.

Interest rates do not live in a vacuum. We've been living in a precarious economic environment for several years now. The reason the Fed has kept interest rates down is because as a country, we have grown to live on debt.

We buy almost everything on debt. We borrow money for our cars and we borrow money for our homes. Most of us have credit card debt. Many of us finance our furniture. We are financing *everything*. Not to mention the astronomical $1.4 trillion debt our youth and parents are accruing on college/higher education debt!

Americans in Debt

Most Americans live on some form of debt. There are ways to finance just about everything.

Like I mentioned earlier, a lot of people I speak to are hoping the government will slowly raise interest rates...

When the Fed raises interest rates, that means the banks will charge more on mortgages, car loans, credit cards, etc. If the Fed raises the interest-bearing loan rate by a quarter or half percent, the bank might give you another quarter percent in your CD.

This won't make much difference in your life.

But if the bank is *giving* you more, if they're giving you a quarter percent, a half percent, or even a full percent in your CD, the likelihood is that your mortgage, your car loan, and your credit card rates will triple.

That's a difference you will feel. Believe me.

Banks always give away less than they take, so to speak. They have to. After all, it's their business.

How Many of Us Qualify?

Not only that, but who gets low interest rates in America?

Only the people with credit scores higher than 740-760.[12]

Statistically, most people do not have a credit score that high . . . meaning if interest rates go up, banks will be able to charge even more.

When interest rates go up, it's not a question of earning more . . . it's a question of how much more people will have to pay.

The Fed has kept interest rates down for so long (and will continue to do so) because increasing them would be devastating to so many Americans — and devastating to our economy.

Banks Love Low-Interest Rates

Banks don't want the Fed to increase interest rates either.

Why?

It's bad for business.

Banks love low interest rate environments because they make it easy to advertise.

"Bank with us! We can get you a 15-year mortgage at 3.17% interest!"

But, like we just discussed, who really gets that rate? People with a score higher than 740-760. Do you think a lot of people have scores that high?

Most people have lower credit scores, meaning the bank can ask for 5% to 7% or more for that loan. It advertises a low interest rate to get us in the door, runs our credit, and slaps on a high interest rate. The bank's rate with the Fed remains the same, meaning it makes a much bigger profit on low credit score clients.

Banks love low interest rate environments.

A Tightrope Balancing Act

A lot of people I talk to want to wait until interest rates increase to sell their CDs. But the government can't raise interest rates because we're all living off debt. Raising interest rates would tank the economy.

If people start shelling out more money each month for their mortgages, car loans, and credit card debt, they won't have any money to spend and put back into the economy.

It's a tightrope balancing act.

How would it affect you if your car loan went up $150 a month? What would happen if your adjustable mortgage or home equity line of credit went up by $200 a month?

What about the people that carry credit card debt? You may be spending the same monthly payment on your credit card, but the balance is getting bigger.

If you are spending more of your monthly income on your debt, you're spending less, meaning you're putting less money into the economy. Like I said, this is a tightrope balancing act that benefits the banks most of all! (What a shocker, huh?)

The Fed simply can't raise interest rates, and they haven't been able to for a while. It has been many years since a retiree could feel good knowing their money was getting 5% or 7% in a CD, and I don't see that happening again in the foreseeable future. Frankly, I don't see that happening in our lifetime. The economy couldn't sustain it.

That's why (unlike in the past) so many retirees have taken on the risk of Wall Street. They see no other option.

But just what will that risk mean to your *Life, Safety & Security*? What will it mean to your lifestyle and to your *Peace of Mind*?

Chapter Six:

Market Losses and Market Vulnerability

Two Types of Phone Calls

The number one reason why people are financially unprepared for retirement is because of market volatility.

After the 2008 crash happened, I got two kinds of phone calls.

"Josh, thank you so much for helping us protect our money. So many of our friends are not able to retire now, and we are grateful to be able to retire."

"Thank you, I appreciate the phone call," I would reply. "I really do, but I can't tell you that I knew the market crash would be so devastating. It was simply prudent advice as you were nearing retirement and losses would have taken years to recoup. I'm so glad we met, and that you implemented your Safe & Secure Wealth Compounded plan."

When their money is protected against a major market downturn, the gratitude people have is incredible . . . and it makes me feel good.

There was another similar situation I have to mention. In 2008, before I was independent, I was with a financial group.

One day, I was talking to Howard, the head of the group, in the lobby of our office. We were talking when someone walked in the door.

I recognize this guy. I know who he is. He's one of Howard's clients.

He didn't push me away, but walked right past me, and grabbed Howard. He gave him a bear hug, kissed him on the cheek, and gratefully thanked him.

He looked at Howard and said, "Thank you so much."

"What did I do?" Howard asked.

"Thank you so much for making me move my money from the market. You kept it safe. I would have lost almost everything, and you really saved our family. Thank you so much."

Howard's response was exactly like mine. "Hey, I didn't know the crash would be this bad. I can't take credit for that. It was simply the wise and prudent thing to do."

I was with a financial group that followed the exact same principles that I did, safe and secure financial planning. That's why I was with them.

In my career as a funeral director, people expressed their gratitude for my help on a daily basis. It was emotionally difficult to deal with people's pain every day, but knowing I was making a positive impact in the lives of others was a powerful motivator for me to go back to work the next day to help those in need.

In the financial field, I don't expect that type of emotional positive feedback, and that's OK. I know without a doubt, that by providing Safety and Security to people's financial lives, I am still making that positive impact. That is still just as important to me today as it was back then.

Being Reactive

During that time, I also got a phone call from people who lost so much.

Remember that couple I mentioned earlier in this book? They met with me about six months before the 2008 crash, but never implemented my Safe & Secure strategies.

Marsha called me on the verge of tears and told me that they had lost 45% of their money. She was 63, I believe, and he was 64 when I met them. Now, he was 65. He had wanted to retire at 65, but he couldn't because they'd lost almost half of their money.

"What should I do, Josh?" She said.

I felt horrible because I couldn't help her. I didn't have a magic wand (still don't). There was no way I was going to be able to recapture 45% of the money they lost at age 64 and 65.

Cost of Recovery	
Loss	**% Needed to Get Even**
-20%	+25%
-25%	+33%
-35%	+54%
-50%	+100%

They were not proactive. Being reactive is devastating, because you cannot recapture your lost money. If they would have simply taken 40% of their money and implemented one of my plans, they would have been dramatically better off.

It's painful to know that there were a lot more people on the reactive side of the coin . . . a lot more, who weren't prudent with their savings. It's going to happen again. People are just shortsighted, or they are brainwashed by Wall Street's advertising that the market will always be there for them. Or, they're blinded by, forgive me to say, normal human greed. I don't mean that in a bad way; like I said earlier, it's just part of who we are!

Investor Psychology Cycle

Most Americans who invest in the market fall victim to the Investor Psychology Cycle.

Here's how it works. When the market is up, there's optimism. As the market continues to climb, that optimism changes to excitement, and then to thrill, and then to euphoria.

But when the market starts to go down, investors feel anxiety and then denial. As it continues to fall, fear and desperation start to kick in. Finally, panic, capitulation, and despondency take over.

And when the market goes back up, the cycle begins all over again.

The #1 rule of investing in the market is to buy low and sell high . . . yet most investors are led not by logic, but by emotion. It's this emotion that causes them to make mistakes.

When we implement safe money strategies, we take the emotion out of the decision-making process. You, yes _you_, can protect your money from the psychological roller-coaster of the market. In fact, so many people tell me that they want to get off that ride, but like an addictive drug, _they can't let go_, they stay, and stay until it's too late.

Investor Psychology Cycle

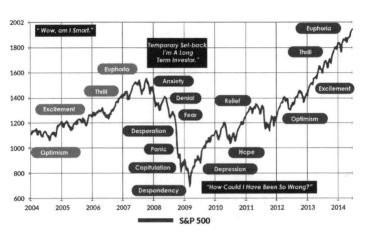

S&P 500

Why?

The Opposite of Common Sense

I don't understand, frankly, how logical, intelligent people get caught up in the frenzy of a volatile market.

The whole point of investing in the market is to grow your money so that you can eventually take it out and use it, right?

But then, as it gets higher and higher, you don't want to have it safer so it will be there for you when you need it. It's weird...it's the opposite of common sense.

I compare it a little bit (maybe more than a little) to gambling.

Personally, I don't like to gamble. As a matter of fact, gambling makes me nervous! However, when I was younger I used to play a little bit of blackjack, either on a cruise or in Vegas (I've attended a lot of financial conferences in Vegas). I saw it more as a social thing. I had a budget, played a few hands, had a drink, and talked to some people — But I can't stand losing money. Spending money, oh, I love to do that. Spending money on my wife, my kids, and my grandkids I love, but losing money, that *freaks me out*.

Anyway, I would sit down with $50 or $100 at the blackjack table. I always chose blackjack because at least there, unlike craps or other tables, I could do the math.

But like I said, I really hate losing money, so every time I would win a hand I would take whatever the winnings from that hand were, and I would put it in my pocket.

I always took my winnings off the table. Always!

And I never added money. If my limit was $50 that night, that's all I would play with. If I lost that money, I would walk away immediately.

But whatever I'm winning, I'm putting in my pocket. If I lose my $50 and walk away, maybe I'll end up with $50 in my pocket. Maybe I'll even end up with $100. Whatever the amount, I would always take my winnings off the table.

This is exactly how we should treat the market. Invest, by all means, but there are times when the market is up, take your winnings off the table.

"Well, when it starts to go down I'll take my money out," is something I hear often.

(Hey, if you know the secret for "Timing the Market," I'm all ears.)

But most of us don't do that. Most of us continue to gamble, fighting to "get even."

Just take a look at history. When the market started crashing in 2007, millions of people didn't take their money out. They waited and waited, hoping it was going to come back.

The wisest money managers in the country didn't see the 2008 crash coming. They didn't see the 2000 crash coming, either.

And I feel quite certain they won't see it the next time either...

Do You Have Everything You Need?

I don't know when the next market crash is coming. It could be in 5 months, it could be in 5 years. I don't know when, but I am fairly confident another crash is coming.

And when it happens, it's going to happen very quickly. It happened quickly in both 2000 and 2008, so why wouldn't we think it's going to happen quickly the next time around? (And it's not just about the next crash, it is cyclical, and will happen more than a few times during your lifetime.)

We are currently in a significant debt bubble. Historically, the larger the disparity between the debt and the increase in the market, the higher probability there is of a greater decline, just as it did in 2000 and 2008.

NYSE Investor Credit and the Market

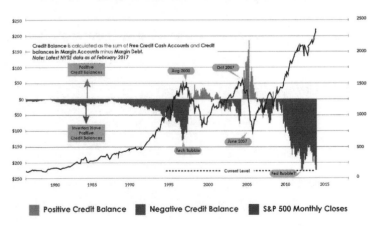

Positive Credit Balance   Negative Credit Balance   S&P 500 Monthly Closes

Like I said, it's not a matter of *if* another market crash is coming, it's a matter of *when*.

So, you need to ask yourself this: Do you need *more* to live the lifestyle you want to live in retirement? Or do you want to be sure you have what you need?

Which is more important?

Most of us have that, "I just want a little more" mentality. It's just part of our humanity but, frankly, I don't understand it. I simply want to know that I'm going to have enough money to enjoy my life and do the things I want to do in retirement. It's not a question of how much, it's a question of whether or not it's enough to provide me with the lifestyle I want to live.

Will I be able to go on vacation?

Will I be able to spend money on my grandchildren?

Most of us lose money in the market because we simply want more. Not because we need it, but because we want it.

Is the risk of losing 45% of your savings really worth it?

Perhaps most importantly . . . Will you have Peace of Mind?

Nothing became clearer to me from my career as a funeral director than the importance of having peace of mind as we grow older. As I often say, there is no substitute for our life's experiences.

Losses and Recovery

The 2008 crash should have been a wake-up call, right?

Unfortunately, most Americans seem to have a short-term memory.

If you're anywhere between the age of 50 and 65, and you are saving money in a 401k or any type of qualified retirement plan, you probably remember that the market went down in 2000, 2001 and 2002.

You also probably remember that the market went back up in 2003 and 2004, and everything seemed hunky-dory again. Everything was just fantastic!

But then, right before everyone got back to where they were after the downturn from 2000 to 2002, in 2008 the market crashed again.

The chart above shows the history of the S&P 500, from January 7, 2000 to December 21, 2009. During that time, the index dropped an average 355.2 points, or -24.18%. That's why 2000 to 2009 is considered **The Lost Decade**.

S&P 500

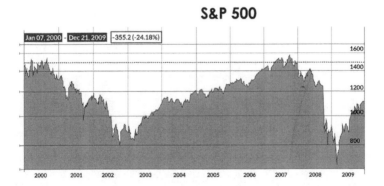

Now, it's nine years later, and people seem to have forgotten.

"Well, everything's doing great right now. Why should I move my money? Everything is fine."

I find it somewhat shocking when people who are close to retirement tell me they want to protect their money and then say;

"Well, I think we have another year before a downturn."

So, they choose to wait!

REALLY? Wait for what? Wait to start losing money?

Being proactive protects you from losses...and the mathematics of having to recapture that money.

I didn't know the market was going to collapse by 45 percent; I was simply being prudent. I was simply being safe and secure.

Unfortunately, because of our human nature, we often want *more*. But if you understand losses and recovery, you may re-think your desire to keep all your money at risk in the market.

For example, if you lose 20% in the market, it takes *25%* just to get back to even. That's a huge lost **opportunity cost**.

Losses and Recovery

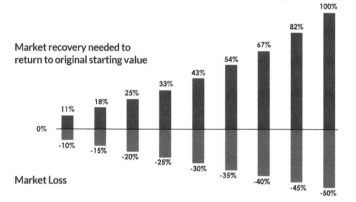

Market recovery needed to return to original starting value

Market Loss

This graphic illustrates the growth you would need to get back to your starting value. For example, If you start with $100,000 and lose 20%, as shown in column 3, your new starting value would be $80,000. The percentage of growth needed to return to the original $100,000 is 25%, but the dollar amount $20,000, is the same. Similarly, If you start with $100,000 and lose 50%, as shown in the last column your new starting value would be $50,000. The Percentage of growth needed to return to the original $100,000 is 100%, but the dollar amount $50,000, is the same.

Securities?

Some of us think our money is safe in the market because our assets are diversified.

The familiar concept of **asset diversification** consists of a 70/30 or 60/40 portfolio made up of a mix of stocks, bonds, and mutual funds.

But real asset diversification includes tax diversification and doesn't only include securities. Stocks, bonds, and mutual funds are all securities, meaning the money inside these types of accounts is at risk.

Let me ask you a question: Why are stocks, bonds, & mutual funds called securities? Is there anything actually _**secure**_ about them?

I wonder which marketing genius came up with the brilliant idea of calling Wall Street financial instruments "Securities."

Wealth Compounding Strategies

What's an opportunity cost?

An opportunity cost is the loss of a potential benefit because another course of action was chosen.

In 2008, the value of the market fell by almost half. Americans who had invested lost 45% of their savings. As soon as that money was lost, it stopped earning interest. It stopped growing. It stopped adding to the account's compound interest curve.

That's why I believe, very strongly, in a Wealth Compounding financial plan as the foundation to any comprehensive plan.

And I've believed in it for a very long time.

Early in my career, from 2002 to 2007, I used to do financial planning seminars. I used to really enjoy it, too. When I was giving these financial planning seminars, I would talk to people about the market.

I've mentioned this already . . . I didn't know the market was going to crash in 2008. Nobody knew that. But when I gave these seminars, in the years before the crash, I spoke about safe money strategies. I was speaking with people in their fifties and sixties, close to retirement, about the same financial strategies I articulate today.

This is my philosophy: The older we get, the closer to retirement, the more important it is to protect a portion of our dollars. It's simply prudent.

Does anyone disagree with that?

I don't know exactly when the market it going to crash again . . . do you?

More importantly, if you can accomplish saving your money efficiently so that you will have the liquidity, tax efficiency, and income to provide you with the lifestyle you want, without all the risk Wall Street has convinced you that you need to have, wouldn't you take the path of less risk?

The Big Short

I just said that nobody knew the 2008 crash was going to hit...

That's not exactly true.

Have you seen *The Big Short*?

It was a movie that came out in 2015 about a handful of people that predicted the crash. Here we are, facing a huge upcoming financial crisis, and literally only a few people saw it.

One was a man who was a physician by trade, who had Asperger's and had social issues, yet had the mathematical insight to see it long before anybody else did. He worked underneath a huge financial institution that told him he was crazy.

Another guy from a subsection of the financial institution, again, told Morgan Stanley, "Something's going to happen here."

They simply said, "No, everything is fine."

Finally, there were two young kids that, somehow or another, saw it as well.

But what's amazing is that so few people saw the crash coming. It's stunning.

How many people will foresee the next crash?

My guess is, not many.

And when that day comes, would you rather be like my mom, someone who has never had to worry about her retirement income?

Or would you rather be like Marsha, someone who didn't take my prudent advice, and calls me *after* the crash, desperate to regain everything she just lost?

Chapter Seven:

The Last Straw

Have you ever heard of the board game, *The Last Straw?*

The idiom, "The straw that broke the camel's back," is derived from the proverb "It is the last straw that breaks the camel's back." The proverb illustrates a seemingly small or mundane action that, after the growing effect of small actions, causes an unforeseeably large and immediate reaction.[13]

When I was a young, my sisters and I would play *The Last Straw* on Saturday afternoons. Each player would take turns putting a straw into his or her side of the camel's basket. Game play continues until one player's straw causes the camel to break in half.

I remember it being a fun game. The tension would grow because you knew the crash was coming.

Who would win? Who would lose?

When would the camel's back break?

Is the Market Overvalued?

That's not so different from today's financial market.

You know the crash is coming. The tension is growing.

Who will win? (Wall Street.)

Who will lose? (Investors.)

When will the market's back break?

What will the straw be that finally breaks this market's back?

Can you tell me what it was that set off the 2000 tech bubble collapse? OR the 2008 market crash? Was it a particular incident? Did you see it coming? Did you get out in time?

Or, was it a seemingly minor or routine action, which caused an unpredictably large and sudden reaction, because of the cumulative effect of small actions?

Dow Jones Historical Price Graph
December, 1999 - December, 2017

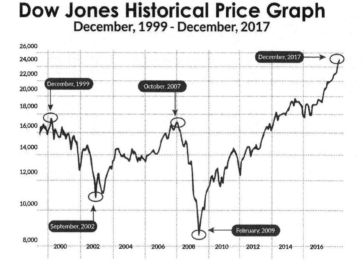

Just as it was in 2000 and 2008, most experts will admit today's market is significantly overvalued. Robert Schiller's CAPE (Cyclically Adjusted Price Earnings – a.k.a Schiller P/E) is the valuation measurement given to the S&P 500. At the end of 2017, it was 32.44%, the third highest in U.S. History. The two times in history is was higher? In 1929 and 1999, right before the Great Depression and the Dot Com Crash.[14] The U.S. Stock Market's P/E ratio is telling us in no uncertain terms that stocks are usually overvalued.[15]

I don't know when the last straw will come, but it *will* break the market's back. I know it will not be predictable. It will be unforeseen, it will be sudden, and many people will lose a great deal of money.

And it will take a long time to recover.

If you're 40 years old or younger and accumulating wealth, perhaps it's not a big concern to you.

But if you're 55 and above, then saving and protecting your money should be your number one priority. You have been saving money for 25 to 35 years. You cannot afford to lose your hard-earned savings during the next unforeseen market crash.

As a child, *The Last Straw* was fun.

As an adult, playing with your life savings shouldn't be a game!

We are in an overvalued market. What will set off the next market crash? What will be the last straw?

Chapter Eight:

Do You Make These Common Mistakes When Saving Your Money?

I am extremely cautious with my money. Let me tell you one of the reasons why.

Like I mentioned earlier in this book, before I became a financial advisor, I served as a funeral director.

When I was young, I wasn't financially savvy. I worked hard and saved where I could, but I didn't really know a thing about investing and wealth accumulation. I had a 401(k) and a savings account, but that was pretty much it.

At the time, I managed a funeral home owned and operated by a local family. During my tenure, they were bought out by a large funeral corporation and after the acquisition, I quite clearly remember someone from their HR department giving us a speech about the corporate stock. We were enthusiastically told to place the majority our 401(k) holdings in the new company's stock.

I was in my 30s with three young children and like I said, not very financially savvy so, I did exactly what they told me to do; I invested all my money in the corporate stock.

You probably know where this story is headed...

Shortly after I moved all my money, my new employers went bankrupt. The large corporation acquired too many small funeral homes too quickly and overspent.

Needless to say, I lost everything . . . It was very, very painful and I've been very cautious ever since.

Where is the Majority of Your Savings?

Many of us have the majority (if not all) of our savings in a **401(k)** . . . but 401(k)s are risky because they're subjected to market volatility, America's biggest retirement threat.

What is a 401(k) and where does it come from? Do you know?

A 401(k) is an employer-sponsored retirement plan allowing employees to invest a portion of their paycheck.[16]

A 401(k) is an example of a **qualified plan**, a plan that requires pre-tax (or before tax) contributions. Qualified plans give you a tax deduction upfront with the understanding that taxes will be taken when the money is withdrawn from the account.[17]

There are many different types of retirement qualified plans.

403(b): This is a retirement savings plan for specific employees in public-schools and tax-exempt organizations. It's also known as a tax-sheltered annuity (TSA) plan.[18]

TSP (Thrift Savings Plan): Created by the Federal Employee's Retirement Systems Act of 1986, this plan offers 401(k)-like retirement savings benefits to current or retired federal civil service employees.[19]

SEP (Simplified Employee Pension): These plans offer business owners a simplified method of contributing to both their employees' retirement savings as well as their own. Contributions are made to an IRA or Annuity.[20]

Traditional IRA (Individual Retirement Account): An IRA allows you to contribute both pre-tax and post-tax dollars to a retirement savings. Like a 401(k), if you contribute pre-tax dollars the money will grow tax-free, but you will have to pay taxes on your withdrawals.[21]

SIMPLE (Savings Incentive Match Plan for Employees) IRA: This plan allows both employers and employees contribute to an IRA. It's a start-up retirement savings plan, used by small companies who don't currently sponsor a retirement plan.[22]

457 Plan: Another deferred-compensation retirement plan, a 457 is offered to government (and specific non-government) employees. The plan is employer sponsored.[23]

Like I said, there are a lot of qualified retirement savings plans! What do they all have in common? They all require pre-tax contributions!

We've already talked about this, but I think it's important to reiterate that tax-deferred doesn't mean tax-free. You don't pay taxes now, but you will pay taxes later, when it's time to take the money out.

You probably won't know what the tax rate will be when you take it out down the road . . . and you could pay dramatically more in taxes!

A Brief History of the 401(k)

A third of all Americans contribute to a 401(k)[24] . . . but 401(k)'s haven't been around forever. Before they were introduced, the majority of working Americans relied on **pensions** for their retirement savings.

A pension fund is managed by the employer. It is also funded by the employer and paid out, in recurring payments, over the course of the employee's retirement.[25]

Corporate pension plans were first created in 1875 by The American Express Company. The plan was applied to employees who had a) reached age 60, b) been recommended for retirement by a manager, and c) had worked for the company for a least 20 years. If an employee qualified, he would receive half his annual salary.[26]

For nearly a hundred years the pension thrived and was the go-to retirement savings vehicle. In the 1970s, most companies still offered their employee pension plans, but as people started living longer, pensions started becoming too expensive to maintain.

Before long, a solution haphazardly presented itself. In 1978, Congress passed the Revenue Act which altered the tax code. It included a provision that allowed employees to defer compensation from stock options or bonuses.[27] It was called *Tax code section 401.*[28] The law went into effect on January 1, 1980 . . . and it forever changed the way Americans retire. [29]

Who is Ted Benna?

Have you ever heard of a guy named Ted Benna? If not, you should. He changed the way America retires.

In the late 70s, Benna worked for a consultant agency, the Johnson Companies where he helped business owners and employers draft, implement, and run pension plans.[30]

When the Revenue Act passed with Tax code section 401 attached, all that changed. While reading the new legislature, he discovered a section of the new code (section "k") that outlined a tax-break for companies allowing employees to put aside retirement savings.

When Benna saw this, a light bulb went off. He drafted a new retirement savings plan that included the tax benefits of Internal Revenue code 401(k), tacked an employer-match incentive onto the deal, and the rest is history. The first 401(k) was born and Benna was praised and deemed the "Father of the 401(k).[31]"

Were 401(k)s Designed to Replace Pensions?

Today, Benna is singing a different tune.

Not only are 401(k)s subjected to market downturns (2000, 2001, 2008, 2009), but the fees are hefty. If you lose money in your 401(k), does your money manager ever offer to refund his or her fee?

Of course not!

Benna regrets that he's helped Wall Street make even more money, and he isn't the only one. Many of the early proponents of the 401(k) also admit that forecasts used to sell the plan in the beginning were too optimistic.

They also state that it was never designed to replace the pension.[32]

> *"The great lie is that the 401(k) was capable of replacing the old system of pensions."*
>
> **- Gerald Facciani, former head of the American Society of Pension Actuaries.**[33]

...yet that seems to be what it has done.

Take a look at this chart . . . what do you think?

Percentage of private-sector workers
participating in an employment-based retirement plan, by plan type

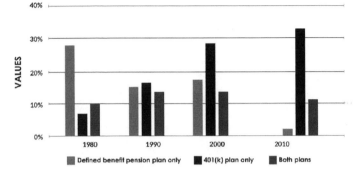

How Useful is Your 401(k)?

When it comes to the way many Americans retire, it's safe to say that 401(k)s have replaced pensions.

But has that replacement been successful?

> **U.S. Census Bureau** researchers, Michael Gideon and Joshua Mitchell, have used tax data (very reliable) to analyze America's retirement future. They looked at tax records from 2012 and confirmed 155 million individual employees and just over 6 million employers. Their calculations determined that only a third of employees are saving in a 401(k) or comparable tax-deferred retirement vehicle. And get this - only 14% of all employers offer a 401(k).[34] How can we say the pension has replaced the 401(k) effectively if only 14% of U.S. businesses offer one?

The data is clear. There are too few Americans saving for retirement . . . and even fewer companies allowing them the opportunity to do so.

Don't get me wrong. A 401(k) can be very useful. Many people have saved a lot of money in their 401(k)s. Without them, many Americans wouldn't save a dime. A 401(k) is a forced savings, leaving people with at least some money saved. That's better than nothing.

But for those of you who do have your savings in a 401(k) (or any qualified savings retirement plan), it's time to start protecting it. The threat of taxes aside, <u>when</u> the market downturns, you could stand to lose so much of what you have worked so hard to save. In 2008, the majority of the population wasn't expecting it, either.

But just as we have helped so many others, my team of advisors and I can help keep your wealth compounding, regardless of taxes or what the market does.

Chapter Nine:

Accumulation vs. Distribution

Are women wiser with money?

There once was a man who loved money more than just about anything.

One day, right before he died, he said to his wife "Now listen. When I die, I want you to put all my money in a box and put it in my casket. I want to take my money with me."

His devoted wife nodded and smiled. She knew her husband well.

At the funeral, she came over with the box and put it in the casket as she had promised. She smiled sweetly as she kissed her fingertips, touched her husband's forehead, and said goodbye.

The funeral director closed the casket and rolled it away.

As the wife watched the casket glide away, a friend said to her, "Did you actually do it?"

The wife replied. "Listen, I'm an honest person. I can't go back on my word. I promised him that I was going to put the money in that casket."

"You really put all that money in there with him!?!?"

"I sure did," said the wife. "I wrote him a check!"

The Sequence of Returns

Remember when I said that market volatility is the single biggest threat affecting the way Americans retire?

There are two phases of your financial life and this chapter is vitally important to your understanding of them.

1. Accumulation Phase: saving and growing your money

2. Distribution Phase: withdrawing and spending your money

If your retirement savings is tied up in the market (often in a qualified plan) and you are beholden to a "rate of return," the mathematics of these two phases are dynamically different.

While we're accumulating money, the sequence of returns does not affect the average rate of return over a certain period of time. However, in the distribution phase of your life, if you're relying on money you have in the market for your income, the **sequence of returns** makes a dramatic difference.

Also called **sequence risk**, the sequence of returns refers to:

> "The risk of receiving lower or negative returns
> early in a period when withdrawals are made
> from an individual's underlying investment.[35]"

Basically, if your portfolio is exposed to market down years at the beginning of your retirement, and you are taking money out, you will run out of money faster. There will be a domino effect driving down your money.

Why?

Because during the accumulation phase, when you're not taking money *out*, the mathematics over a certain period of time remain the same whether the market is going up or going down.

For example, let's say you have an 8% average rate of return (Wow, that would be great!) for 25 years. Regardless of when (during that time) the market was up or down, you would have the same amount of money in your account. You could start in an up year and end in a down year (or vice versa) and it wouldn't make a difference to the amount you have at the end of the accumulation phase.

On the other hand, market performance at the beginning of your distribution phase (when you start taking money out) makes a VERY big difference to the amount of money you can withdraw . . . and for how long it will last for you! If the market goes down at the beginning of your retirement, and then goes up later on, you will lose a significant amount of your wealth . . . and you will potentially run out of money.

But if you invert that sequence of returns (meaning you had high returns in the beginning of the distribution phase and then the market goes down later), you might end up with significantly more money in the market.

To give you a better example of what I'm talking about, take a look at this chart:

Accumulation Period
Starting Value: $100,000 No Distributions

Age	Annual Return	Year End Value	Annual Return	Year End Value
41	-12%	$87,695	29%	$129,491
42	-21%	69,426	18%	152,281
43	-14%	59,707	25%	189,590
44	22%	72,894	-6%	178,404
45	10%	80,136	15%	204,272
46	4%	83,595	8%	221,183
47	11%	92,707	27%	221,124
48	3%	95,210	-2%	274,939
49	-3%	92,155	15%	315,355
50	21%	111,507	19%	372,272
51	17%	130,129	33%	498,737
52	5%	137,836	11%	554,097
53	-10%	123,597	-10%	499,737
54	11%	137,316	5%	526,284
55	33%	182,493	17%	614,174
56	19%	217,167	21%	743,150
57	15%	249,091	-3%	719,305
58	-2%	243,611	3%	738,726
59	27%	309,626	11%	819,247
60	8%	335,262	4%	854,602
61	12%	383,875	10%	936,354
62	-6%	361,226	22%	1,147,022
63	25%	449,727	-14%	986,439
64	18%	528,878	-21%	780,941
65	29%	684,848	-12%	684,848
	8%	$684,848	8%	$684,848

Withdrawal Period
Annual income: 5% of initial balance, and adjusted for annually thereafter

Age	Annual Return	Year End Value	Annual Return	Year End Value
66	-12%	$566,337	29%	$852,571
67	-21%	413,066	18%	967,355
68	-14%	318,927	25%	1,168,029
69	22%	352,432	-6%	1,061,698
70	10%	348,431	15%	1,177,105
71	4%	323,772	8%	1,234,835
72	11%	318,176	27%	1,528,614
73	3%	284,653	-2%	1,452,871
74	-3%	232,143	15%	1,623,066
75	21%	236,215	19%	1,886,771
76	17%	229,644	33%	2,461,500
77	5%	194,417	11%	2,687,327
78	-10%	126,543	-10%	2,375,148
79	11%	90,304	5%	2,450,746
80	33%	68,219	17%	2,808,226
81	19%	27,833	21%	3,344,606
82	15%	0	-3%	3,182,338
83	-2%	0	3%	3,211,664
84	27%	0	11%	3,503,440
85	8%	0	4%	3,594,592
86	15%	0	10%	3,885,017
87	-6%	0	22%	4,685,257
88	25%	0	-14%	3,963,710
89	18%	0	-21%	3,070,398
90	29%	0	-12%	2,622,984
	8%	$0	8%	$2,622,984

Take two hypothetical phases, the accumulation phase where no distributions are made, and the retirement phase, where income is 5% of beginning principal value and adjusted for inflation thereafter. In all cases, the average return was 8%. Note the sequence of hypothetical (but consistent with ranges in the S&P since 1983) returns. (Source: Standard & Poor's) In each phase, we have a sequence of returns, then invert them to look at the implication of how the returns effect the outcome.
During the accumulation phase, regardless of the sequence of returns, what mattered was the average annual return.
Both columns in our accumulation phase resulted in the same number at age 65.
But not so in the retirement phase. In the retirement phase, where negative results occured in the early years, we ran out of money at the age of 81. On the other hand, t our inverted, with the average still being 8%, and we met our needs with more than $2 1/2 million at age 90!
We can "average 8%, take out 5% (with inflation), and still run out of money."

As you can see, Portfolios A and B, both with an 8% average rate of return, end up with the same amount of money at the end of the accumulation phase, regardless of market volatility.

But there is a dramatic difference in the distribution phase:

	Balance After 1st Year	Market Performance at Beginning of Distribution Phase	Ending Balance
Portfolio A	$566,337	Down	$0 at Age 82
Portfolio B	$852,571	Up	$2,622,984 at Age 90

Portfolio A runs out of money at age 82 in this example since it was exposed to market losses early in the withdrawal (or distribution) phase. Thus, the balance for which you are taking money out is driven down (5% in this example).

By contrast, Portfolio B experienced market gains in the beginning and losses at a later date, leaving a much higher balance in the end.

You could get lucky, enter retirement during a market upswing, and have a better opportunity to not run out of money . . . or you could hit a couple of down years at the beginning of your retirement and run out of money much earlier than you had planned.

But it's so much more than numbers, right?

It's the stress and anxiety of not knowing how the market will affect your ability to live the life you want.

Wouldn't it be better to have a plan where, no matter what happens in the markets, the economy, or the world, you can have consistent and predictable retirement income, no matter what the market does?

As far as I know, none of us have a crystal ball. At least I know I don't! None of us are going to be able to know when those ups and downs in the market will occur.

Remember my Mom? The market tanked a few years after she retired, but she never had to worry about sequence of returns risk because she had a Wealth Compounding Plan.

Retirement may last for <u>at least 30 years or more</u> . . . meaning the market will experience more than a couple ups and downs. That's reason enough to protect a portion of your wealth!

Will you be one of the lucky few who retires in a market up year, and ends up with excess? Or will you be caught off guard by a market downturn in the first or second year of your retirement and potentially run out of money?

It's crucial to have "ROI."

No, not *Return on your Investment,* as most of us interpret that acronym, but in this context, <u>*Reliability of Income*</u>.

Wouldn't you agree?

Chapter Ten:

What Is Important to You?

My granddaughter loves this story...

Once upon a time there were Three Little Pigs. The first pig built a house with straw while the second pig built his house with sticks.

One day, a Big Bad Wolf saw these two little pigs while they danced and played outside their homes.

He thought, "Hmmm, what a juicy meal they will make!"

He chased the two little pigs and they ran and hid in their houses. The Big Bad Wolf went to the first house made of straw.

He huffed and

He puffed and

He blew the straw house down!

The frightened little pig ran to the second pig's house. The Big Bad Wolf came to the house made of sticks and

He huffed and

He puffed and

He blew the house down!

Terrified, the two little pigs ran to the third pig's house.

The third pig was different than his brothers. Instead of playing in the sun, he took his time building his house. He hired an architect who designed a sturdy house with a strong foundation and a contractor who built his house with brick walls. He built his house strong enough to weather any storm.

The Big Bad Wolf walked up to the third little pig's house. He didn't notice the house was made out of bricks. He simply saw the frightened pigs in the window and remembered how hungry he was. He grinned from ear to ear, revealing a row of sharp, pointy teeth.

He huffed and

He puffed and

...nothing happened.

He tried again, and again, and again. But no matter how hard he tried, he couldn't blow the brick house down.

After a while, the Big Bag Wolf became tired and left the Three Little Pigs alone. They were safe.

The first and second little pigs would have to work hard to rebuild everything they had lost, but the third little pig, because he had taken the time to plan and build a strong house with a strong foundation, he did not. He didn't have to worry about his house, his possessions, or his lifestyle.

They were all safe from the Big Bad Wolf, but only the third little pig was safe from financial loss.

Too many Americans' financial houses are built of straw or sticks. Too many Americans' financial houses will be blown away by taxes or the next market crash. Too many Americans will experience significant financial losses . . . losses that will take years to recover, damaging a person's ability to live the lifestyle they have worked so hard to achieve.

What's Important to You?

What is truly important to you?

Safety?

Growth?

Income?

Liquidity?

Taxation?

Charitable giving?

Leaving money behind for loved ones?

It's different for everyone. What's important to John is likely very different from what's important to Jane.

The things that are important to you can even change over time. What's important to you at age 40 might be completely dissimilar than what's important to you at age 65.

I want you to achieve what's important to you. If I can understand what that is, I can make proper financial recommendations to help get you there.

But first, you need a strong financial house. Decide what's important to you and then build your house around that.

You Need a Strong Financial House

Prosperity and achieving what's important to you depends completely on reliability of income. Reliability of income begins with a strong financial house.

"The success of what you're currently doing is based upon the foundation which immediately precedes it."

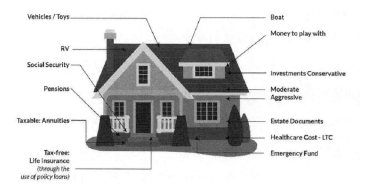

Your Financial House Foundation

Take a look at the image above and make note of the three different levels. Every strong financial house is built in three easy steps:

Step #1: Build Your Foundation

The first thing every house needs is a foundation.

For your financial house, for your foundation, you need to have income you can count on. You need safe investments that will protect you from market downturns. It's also smart to have cash, protection for health care, and solid strategies that create a strong financial foundation to build upon.

Step 2: Take on More Risk

Now it's time to take some risks.

Once you've created a financial foundation for your house, you can take on assets that have more risk. Your foundation is strong, right? Now it can handle the turbulent blows the market will inevitably bring.

Step #3: The Path to Prosperity

Finally, you get to buy some toys.

Because you built a strong foundation, you were able to take on more risk. Now you can afford the fun and meaningful things that you want in your lifestyle. The RV's, the vacation homes, the boats. Now, you have more money for travel and for spoiling your grandchildren. (Spoiling my grandchildren . . . that's my favorite!)

With the right foundation, your chances of surviving a major financial storm dramatically increase. With the right foundation, you can eventually use the least amount of assets to create guaranteed income (more on this later).

All of this, working together, will ultimately lead you to what's important to you. It will lead you to your path of prosperity.

It might mean the ability to travel and see your grandchildren. Or, it might mean the ability to leave a legacy or a charitable gift. Whatever it means, whatever may be important, creating a comprehensive plan around it generates the greatest opportunity for a path to prosperity for you and your family.

If you're ready to learn more, visit <u>www.WealthCompounded.com</u> to schedule your complimentary consultation.

Do You Have a Financial House of Cards?

In 2008, some people lost 50% of their retirement savings. They had worked all those years, saved, and thought they were going to have peace of mind in retirement.

But then they lost a fortune overnight.

Because their plan didn't have a strong foundation, like a house of cards against the wind, their financial house crumbled.

> *"The success of what you are currently doing is based upon the foundation which immediately precedes it."*

To be successful, everything that we do needs a solid foundation on which to grow. If your financial house is built on market investments, when the next big financial storm hits, when the next 2008 comes along, your financial house is going to get blown away.

But if you have a strong foundation, if you have social security, or a pension, or an annuity . . . if you have liquidity, use, and control of your money . . . if you have a will and/or a trust, the overall health of your financial house will be strong.

Once you've created that foundation, you can move forward with confidence. Once you have that confidence, you will provide *Freedom & Flexibility* for your other assets to withstand the ultimate winds to come.

And once you build your assets, once everything in your financial house is working together in harmony, you will be able to have peace of mind and the things that are important to you.

Is There a Perfect Product for Everyone?

Is there a perfect strategy or product?

No. Of course not.

> There is no such thing as a perfect financial strategy or a perfect financial product.

It's about a comprehensive, balanced plan.

For example, you can save safely with CDs, money markets, and/or fixed annuities, but you won't make much, just 1% to 3%. On the other hand, you can stay in the market and take on all the risk. For example, you could make as much as 15% in the market, but as many have before, you could also lose 35%.

There are pros and cons to everything.

Look at an indexing strategy, for example.

The Pros are:

- Protection of principal
- Gains that lock in and cannot be lost.
- Your money grows from where it locked in
- You never have to recover from losses

This could *potentially* be an excellent part of a strategy.

The con to that is that your upside potential is mitigated in some way.

Is that a valuable portion to your overall plan?

It could be. It all depends on what is important to *you*. It all depends on how you've designed your financial house.

Index Funds

I want to take a brief moment to talk about index funds.

A lot of people talk about index funds. John Bogle (sometimes he goes by Jack Bogle), who is the founder of Vanguard Funds, tells us that with index funds, over time, your money will grow with the market returns year after year . . . but the problem with that is, when the market goes down in a Vanguard Index Fund, your money will go down too.[36] And it can go way down. If we look back to 2008, Vanguard Funds followed the S&P, and people lost 37% of their money.[37]

Money managers, Wall Street publications, and many people talk about average rate of return, but like I said in an earlier chapter, it isn't where the market is today, it's where the market will be when you need it. If the market goes down (or has gone down) when you need it, that could be devastating to you.

So . . . how can you get those index gains, and understand how to protect yourself at the same time?

A Guaranteed Foundation of Income

Personally, as I've said, I'm very big on having peace of mind. I'm very, very big on peace of mind.

And it's not only me.

So many people have told me the comfort that having financial peace of mind brings to them. My goal for the people I work with is to create a comprehensive financial plan, a solid financial house, that will give them peace of mind most have worked so hard to achieve.

I'm not here to provide any single product. I can't emphasize that enough, because we are all different, because we all have different priorities, different things that are important to us, we *each* need to have a strategy to meet your personal financial situation. But one thing we all need, is our *Wealth Compounded*.

There isn't one single product, strategy or plan that's best for everyone. There simply isn't.

> If we start with a comprehensive plan, with a strong financial foundation, a foundation of guaranteed income, we can achieve not only peace of mind in retirement, but prosperity. We can live the life and lifestyle we have worked so hard to achieve.

Once we have a guaranteed foundation of income, our other assets can be given more freedom and flexibility. And from there, we are able to focus on what's important to you.

By building a comprehensive plan, we are able to reach a path of prosperity. Ultimately, you will be able to achieve what's important to you in your lifetime.

Whether that's leaving a legacy for your family, creating a charitable gift for others, buying that boat you've had your eye on for a decade, or my favorite, spending time with and spoiling my grandchildren, building a strong financial house will ensure you can live the lifestyle for which you've worked so hard.

Is the foundation of your house made of straw and sticks?

Or is your foundation made of bricks?

Chapter Eleven:

What Are Your Goals?

What are your financial goals?

Achieving what's important to you means first identifying your goals . . . but most Americans never stop to ask themselves that question. They think of financial **tools**, when instead they should be focusing on **strategies** that will help them to achieve those **goals**.

What are those tools? We'll get to that in a bit.

First, we need to understand your *goals*. Otherwise, how can we pick the right strategies? And if we don't know the right strategies, how can we possibly know the right tools?

The 3 Steps to Identifying the Right Financial Plan

Step #1: Identify Your Goals

Step #2: Create the Right Strategy

Step #3: Pick the Best Tools to Reach Your Goals

Step #1: Identify Your Goals

The first step to compounding your wealth is to **Identify Your Goals**. How can you possibly pick the right tools if you don't know what your long-term (and even short-term) objectives are? Your goals, and the right strategies, are much more important than the tools.

Don't get me wrong, we need tools. Like ingredients for a recipe, we need tools just as we need flour to bake a cake. But before we shop for the ingredients, we first need to know what kind of cake to bake (goals), and how to bake it (strategies), right?

Goals first, tools last.

Is your goal to retire in two years?

Maybe you want additional retirement income to protect your lifestyle?

Do you want the freedom to travel?

Or is your goal to never be a burden on your children?

Whatever it is, identifying your financial goals must come first. Once we identify your goals, creating the right strategy becomes much easier.

Step #2: Create the Right Strategy

Once you've identified your goals, it's time to **Create the Right Strategy**.

That's where I come in. It's my job to develop strategies to safeguard those goals and help you compound your wealth.

Everyone is different, and like I've said before, I'm not a one-trick pony. I believe, very strongly, that a financial strategy should be unique and specific. Identifying your unique goals allows me to create unique and specific strategies that will help you achieve those goals.

For example, if your goal is to retire in two years, maybe we need to develop an income strategy you can count on. Or, if your concern is market fluctuation, then we need to work to protect a portion of the wealth you've worked so hard to save. Perhaps taxation is an issue and a strategy to mitigate taxes for you and your family is most important.

Throughout this book, we've covered the potential effects that market fluctuation, inflation, and taxes may have on your wealth. If your goal is to protect your money from those threats, maybe we need to focus on strategies that protect against market downturns, inflation, and diversify your tax portfolio.

Depending on your goals, there may be healthcare, legacy, and estate strategies to consider.

The right strategy (or strategies) become very clear when you know what your financial goals are.

Step #3: Pick the Best Tools

Finally, after you've identified your goals and have a strategy tailored to those goals, you can move on to the last step of the process, **Pick the Best Tools**.

Like I mentioned at the beginning of the chapter, most Americans focus on this step first. Therefore, most of us are likely very familiar with many of the tools we have at our disposal.

There are stocks, bonds, ETFs, and mutual funds. There's gold, real estate, annuities and tax-advantaged life insurance policies. There are 401(k)s, IRAs, Roth IRAs, CDs, and good old-fashioned savings accounts. There are even more tools out there and at our disposal . . . There are so many to choose from, that doing so can sometimes feel overwhelming. It's no wonder most people simply follow the mold and sign up for their company's 401(k) without batting an eye!

> When we identify our goals and create the right strategy, picking the best tools becomes much, much easier.

It's All About Your Goals

Ultimately, it isn't about the tools, it's about your goals. It's about what you want out of life. It's about what's important to you.

So many of us are hung up on the type of tool we're using. We have no strategy in place and yet we assume that we're picking the right tools and adequately planning for the future.

Without the right strategy, compounding your wealth becomes very, very difficult and almost impossible. Compounding your wealth (and keeping it compounding) requires coordination *and* the right tools. There's no way around it.

Strategy, like we've talked about, is personalized.

It isn't too uncommon that I receive a call from someone who has responded to my radio ad and the first thing they say is...

"Tell me what you have to offer, Josh."

In my opinion, that is certainly not the right way to go about it. How can I recommend a strategy, or tools, without first knowing your personal situation, what your goals are, and what's important to you?

So, for some foundational knowledge, in the next several chapters, I'm going to talk about a few strategies and some of the proven tools that have helped many of my clients reach their financial goals.

Chapter Twelve:

High Net Worth Strategies

Do you have a net worth of over $5 million? Or maybe you'd like to get there some day?

If you do, keep reading. This chapter of the book is written especially for you.

In football, the quarterback is one of the most important positions on the field. He touches the ball on almost every single offensive play, strategizes with the coaching staff, and coordinates with his teammates to accomplish the single-most important goal of the day: To win the game.

A little earlier in the book, I told you about a client worth over $100 million who was without an Estate Plan. It was something he knew he needed to do . . . yet he simply hadn't.

"You know, Josh, the easiest thing to procrastinate on is something that's not knocking at your door."

A wise man, indeed.

This client is worth $100 million, and if he doesn't create an Estate Plan, the government stands to take quite a lot of it when he passes.

Let me back up a moment. Everyone has an Estate Plan, most just don't know it! If you have not implemented one yourself, then the government will implement theirs for you, and I can assure you, that will mean the IRS and attorneys take a big piece of your pie.

> Have you been working hard your entire life, to give a large portion of your money to the government?

Is that what you want?

There are a number of strategies (different types of trusts, charitable giving, generational skipping, etc.) you can employ to protect your money, your *legacy*, from Uncle Sam's clutches.

Now, back to my $100 million client . . . personally, I do not have the specialty to handle a client of such wealth on my own. Most of my clients have a net worth of $1 to $5 million.

But like a quarterback, I have a team of attorneys, CPAs, and other advisors with whom I coordinate, that *specialize* in estate planning. And like that quarterback, I will work with my team to accomplish your single-most important goal: keeping your money safe (while legally and ethically keeping more of your money with you than with the IRS).

And to close the loop on this client . . . he finally decided to take the plunge and procrastinate no more. Together with a team of specialized professionals, we are working to create a plan so that his money stays safe (and protected from excessive taxation) for generations, and he will be able to control its direction, both for his family and the charities that are important to him.

But estate planning isn't just for the wealthy; virtually everyone should have a trust to protect their assets. You've worked hard to Compound Your Wealth! You should keep it safe!

If you don't have an estate plan or a trust, visit <u>www. WealthCompounded.com</u> to schedule an appointment and get started!

Another Strategy for the Wealthy

Leveraged Compound Arbitrage (LCA) is a cash accumulation strategy that has historically been reserved for clients with an average personal net worth of $10 million or more.

However, through unique relationships and partnerships, I have produced an exclusive program <u>available to clients with varying levels of net worth.</u> It is designed for **individuals, privately held companies, business owners**, and **501(c)(3)** foundations that have an investment fund and want to achieve freedom from taxation AND protect themselves against stock market crashes).

How does the LCA strategy work?

It uses a proprietary index account that is correlated with the S&P 500 and has a 0% floor stop loss feature, protecting clients against market crashes.

Several components of this strategy also provide favorable Federal and State tax treatment due to utilizing certain life insurance-based products. This is especially important in light of the most recent changes in the 2018 Federal tax law.

Why should you take a serious look at this strategy?

<u>Let's do the math.</u>

The financial results that our clients experience are indisputable because I don't use economic philosophy or speculation. We ONLY show the irrefutable mathematical outcomes that our strategy produces, plus our software has the ability to show an apples-to-apples comparison using ANY investment alternative in the market.

Once you see the indisputable, *irrefutable* mathematical outcomes that our strategy can produce, <u>if you qualify</u>, you'll want to have this safe, tax-advantaged strategy as part of your plan.

Chapter Thirteen:

The Case Against This Popular Tool

M y mother is currently 85 and has been retired for 20 years. Her goal was to never worry about the market eroding her money and having income in retirement with absolute peace of mind, and thanks to this tool, she achieved her goal.

Like we talked about, the goal, and the strategy to achieve that goal, are more important than the tool. The tool is an ingredient, but accomplishing the goal is what's important.

And when it comes to goals, are we really that different?

I talk to a lot of different people from different parts of the country . . . and the more I do, the more I realize that we're not so dissimilar. We come from different places and have different backgrounds, but more often than not it's our family that's important to us, and our financial goals revolve around them.

People want to live the lifestyle that is important to them.

Whether that means paying for their children's college education and/or weddings, going away on vacations, visiting your grandchildren (my favorite because they are so cute!), or spending quality time with your spouse, having the peace of mind to do these things is what's most important to all of us.

My job is ultimately to learn what's specifically important to you and help you with the solutions and create the strategies to get you there. Money is really just a vehicle to help us to reach the things that are important to us in our lives.

That's what I want to help you to do. I want to provide you with the foundation of education so that we can take the next step, and then the next step, so you can ultimately be successful.

After all,

> *"The success of what you are currently doing is based upon the foundation which immediately precedes it!"*

Living Proof

I just had a call with an interesting fellow. He's 63 and wants to put his money in an annuity.

Let me start off by saying, this isn't typical. Most people don't call me asking about annuities.

But this guy knew what he wanted. His mother is 92, his father is 97, and they still live in their home. Aside from social security, the only money that they have is the income from their annuities.

He went on to tell me that he's worked hard, and he's worked hard to save his money.

"Look, my parents bought their annuities 30 years ago when they were close to my age. All their other money has run out. Their money from their annuities has been a constant flow of income. They can count on it."

I sat back and listened.

"If my mom lives to be 105, that money is going to keep going. That's what I want. I want to know my income will be there for me."

Pretty hard to argue with his logic. He has seen how it has benefited his parents, and now he wants the same safety and security for himself.

For some reason (I know the reason, just ask me), many people feel that annuities are not a good investment, but remember it's not about the tool, it's about what that tool can do for you.

Of course, Wall Street will tell you Annuities aren't good. Annuities are tools from a life insurance company, therefore Wall Street doesn't make money from them! Do you really think your Money Manager is going to suggest you put your money somewhere they <u>don't</u> make a commission? Think about that.

My Mom Didn't Lose a Penny

There really is no substitute for life experience.

When my mom retired in 1997, she purchased two index annuities . . . and her money was protected from day one.

In 2000, 2001, 2002, she was in retirement in the distribution phase of her life. The market went down for three years in a row she didn't lose a penny. Remember sequence of returns? If her money had been in the market, she would likely be in a very different position today.

My mother purchased those annuities in 1997. As other people were trying to recapture their losses and get back to where they were in 2000, my mom was way ahead of the game. She didn't lose money and she didn't lose any sleep over the market's ups and downs.

Is an Annuity Right for You?

We all don't know what we don't know.

Wouldn't you agree?

Before we begin, let me start off by saying that annuities aren't right for everyone. If you're younger than 50, then there may be other strategies and tools more appropriate for you.

But if you've saved up quite a bit of money, and you want a Safe and Secure financial foundation for your retirement, an annuity may be an excellent part of your strategy.

So many people just don't understand anything about annuities, let alone the differences between them. That's why I believe very strongly in education. I have found that people who are willing to learn, create the greatest benefits for themselves.

Now that we got that out of the way, let's talk about how annuities work. There are different types of annuities, with very different features. One may be right for your neighbor, and a different one might be right for you.

Let's start here. Are you familiar with the fact that an annuity is only a financial vehicle of a life insurance company?

I'd say only about 30% of people I speak to can answer "Yes."

An annuity is simply a financial product of a life insurance company. If you go to a bank and purchase an annuity, the bank will purchase it from a life insurance company. Annuities are only issued through a life insurance company.

So, my next question is: How safe do you believe your money is with a life insurance company?

A lot of people hem and haw, when I ask them this question.

Well...

"It depends on the ratings."

"I'm not really sure, but I think it's safe? "

This is the general consensus, but if we look at history, specifically the 2008 market crash, we get a very clear understanding.

On September 15, 2008, Lehman Brothers went bankrupt.[38] Bear Sterns was sold for two dollars a share. At that time, that was less than a tenth of the firm's market price.[39] Goldman Sachs, Wells Fargo, and Bank of America all had to be bailed out. JPMorgan Chase alone was given $25 billion by the United States government.[40]

You probably remember hearing about the Lehman Brothers bankruptcy and the big bank bailouts...

But did you hear of any life insurance companies that had to be bailed out at that time?

The $180 Billion Bail Out

When I ask my clients that question, most say, "No."

But every once in a while, somebody says, "Hmmm, AIG?"

In late 2008, the government bailed out AIG for a whopping $180 BILLION.[41]

The fact of the matter is that AIG isn't a life insurance company. It is an insurance conglomerate representing many different companies.

For example, they have a casualty company. They're the largest insurer of planes in the world. They have an investment banking division which is the part of their business that got in trouble with the wild bets they were making with Wall Street pre-2008.

They also have an insurance company by the name of American General. American General is a subsidiary of AIG. If AIG was not bailed out, American General would've been sold off as their strongest asset.

I personally have life insurance with American General. Many of my clients have annuities with them, as well. If AIG hadn't been bailed out and American General was sold off as its strongest asset, the only thing that would've changed on my end would have been the name of the life insurance company holding my policy.

The Glass-Steagall Act

Let's back up a moment and talk about the **Glass-Steagall Act**.

Originally, the Banking Act of 1933 gave the Federal Reserve the power to regulate retail banks. The congressional act was enacted after the Great Depression, when almost 5,000 banks closed for four days in 1933. (When those banks re-opened, they gave depositors ten cents on every dollar.) The banks had invested in the stock market, which crashed in 1929. The Banking Act was passed to prevent banks from investing in Wall Street so that the depression would not occur again.[42]

Fast forward 60 years when the Glass-Steagall Act was repealed from 1998 to the year 2000. Sure enough, from 2000 to 2009, we had the worst market crashes in our lifetime, and had a negative rate of return over ten years.

Of course, Wall Street people would like to dispute that, because they don't want regulation. After all, during the 2008 market crash, Main Street lost, but so many on Wall Street made a fortune. I think it's indisputable that the lack of Wall Street regulations led to the debacle we had.

The Legal Reserve System

Unlike Wall Street and the banks, life insurance companies are highly regulated by a system called the **legal reserve**. This system is enforced by each and every state.

Legal reserve means that life insurance companies have to have dollar per dollar in reserves to meet their obligations.

A bank, on the other hand, takes $100 in deposits and loans out $1,000. They can do **fractional lending**.

In 1929, when the stock market crashed, people ran to the banks to get their money because they knew the bank didn't have all their money. That's where the phrase "Run on the bank" comes from. People ran to the bank to get their money.

Life insurance companies cannot do that. They cannot participate in fractional lending. They're not legally allowed to.

Aside from their dollar per dollar in reserves, on top of their reserves, they have to have 3-7% surplus money in their account. There are reinsurance companies as well, companies that take on a certain amount of a life insurance company's liabilities.

Almost everything is a liability to a life insurance company. The death benefit, the annuity payout, the disability payout, long term care, anything like that. They are all liabilities on their books.

Are You Familiar with Guarantor Funds?

Also, each and every state has what's called the **guarantor fund**.

In Florida, we have the Florida State Guarantor Fund (They all have a similar name in each state).

What this means is that each state is going to back up a certain amount of your benefit, or cash value, from a life insurance company. Cash values, death benefits, long-term care, annuity cash values and payouts, disability insurance, and long-term care are guaranteed, to a certain dollar amount. Whatever life insurance policy you have, it's backed up by the state, up to a certain dollar amount.

This is what I call a last bastion of security. If your money is with a large life insurance company, you won't need this extra line of protection, but it's good to know that it's there.

Wouldn't you agree?

Of course, a lot of people are familiar with the FDIC (the Federal Deposit Insurance Corporation) and know that, frankly, it's underfunded. The federal government can print money, whereas states can't. As a matter of fact, most states are broke.

You might ask,

"How in the world can a state guarantee even one penny of your money in your annuity or your life insurance policy? How can they do that?"

Most people don't know the answer.

I have more than a few life insurance policies. Every time I put money into one of my life insurance policies (or any life insurance product, like an annuity, for example), the insurance company has to give the state a piece of that money. It's already built into all the costs.

Basically, the state is saying to the insurance company, for the pleasure of doing business in our state, you have to give us the money to guarantee our consumers are taken care of. The states don't have the money, but they get the money from the insurance companies.

That's a rock-solid guarantee.

The Four Different Types of Annuities

Now that you know how safe your money is within a life insurance company, let's talk about the four different types of annuities. Each has a different purpose. Some are likely better for you than others.

Some have no expense and are straightforward, and some are expensive and a bit complicated. If you die, some allow you to pass the balance on to your heirs, and some don't.

For example, if you purchase an Immediate Annuity, and you die prior to your principal being paid back to you, the insurance company keeps the balance. Unfortunately, these types of annuities have given annuities a bad name. Many people think all annuities work like this, but they don't.

Each annuity serves a different purpose. You may discover that there aren't any annuities that are right for you, and that's OK. My job is to guide you through the retirement planning process by introducing you to your options and discovering what will work best for you, to fulfill your goals. Like I've said before, I don't believe in one-size-fits-all.

#1: Single Premium Immediate Annuity

The oldest type of annuity is called the **Single Premium Immediate Annuity**, or an **SPIA**. It's very simple to understand. Just think "pension." You give the insurance company your money, and they give you a stream of income, based upon your age, for as long as you live, no matter how long you live.

The downside to that is that you're giving up all liquidity, use, and control of your money. Plus, it's an irrevocable decision.

Personally, I don't like to give up liquidity, use, and control unless I must, or if it's part of a comprehensive strategic plan. A single premium immediate annuity is something that's usually only recommended to someone who is looking for the highest stream of income. Someone in their late 70s or maybe early 80s who isn't worried about leaving money behind.

This type of annuity only fits into very specific situations and is mostly beneficial for older individuals. It's very simple to understand, it's just pure longevity insurance. You give the insurance company the money, and they give you a stream of income just like a pension or social security. The problem is that when you die with a single premium immediate annuity, the insurance company keeps all the money. If you die the next day, the day after you purchase the annuity, they keep all the money. It can be guaranteed for a husband or wife, but nonetheless, when you die, they keep the money.

If you die young, the insurance company wins. If you die old, you win.

Personally, I like a win-win for everybody, not for one or the other.

#2: Fixed Annuities

Think "CD's."

When you purchase **Fixed Annuities (FA)**, you give the insurance company your money and tell them you're going to leave it there for five years. They can give you a five-year term and a specific rate of return.

Today if you get a five-year CD, the bank is probably going to give you 1.6% interest or something like that, whereas the insurance company will give you more like 3% on a fixed annuity.

The insurance company will always give you a higher rate of return than a bank will. Like I mentioned earlier in this book, we're not just experiencing historically low interest rates. Many people believe we're in the new low interest rate environment. Yes, they may go up a bit, but they won't be life-changing.

#3: Variable Annuities

Next up are **Variable Annuities**.

What is a variable annuity?

Let's start with the definition of variable.

Variable means it can go up and down, meaning your money goes up and down.

My personal opinion is, if you are getting an annuity, you get it for its Safety and Security, you don't want a variable annuity because it puts your money at risk in the market.

Many people think annuities are expensive. This is a common misconception, emboldened by variable annuities.

The previous annuities we discussed (SPIA and FA) are simple, straightforward, and don't have any fees.

Variable annuities, however, are very expensive. They have the highest fees (administrative fees, mortality and expense fees, trading fees, and rider fees) and can add up to easily 3.5% in costs.

These annuities can have a lot of bells and whistles, so to speak, but they are very, very expensive.

We can get you more Safety, Security, growth, and income in another strategy with *substantially* less fees.

#4: Fixed Index Annuities

The fourth type of annuity is a **Fixed Index Annuity (FIA)** and sometimes you will hear it marketed as a hybrid annuity.

A Fixed Index Annuity puts together some of the best features of the other annuities.

It gives you principal protection from any market downturns.

It has market growth that locks in and resets.

It provides Safe, Secure growth, and can also have a feature to create guaranteed lifetime income that you cannot outlive.

Take a look at this chart.

Hypothetical Historical Example

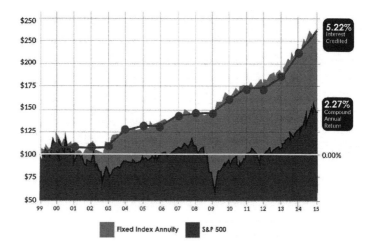

When the market went down in 2000, 2001, 2002, and 2008, I told you that my mom didn't lose any money.

The bottom part of this chart is the S&P 500. The top part of the chart is a fixed index annuity through 2015.

(Later, I'll show you how an FIA strategy has performed through 2017.)

As you can see, when most people were just getting back to even in 2007, my mom was way ahead of the game. When the market crashed in 2008, not only did my mom not lose any money, but you know what else she didn't lose? My mom told me she didn't lose any sleep! She may have had other things to worry about, but she never lost any sleep or worried when the markets were fluctuating or crashing. Imagine having that type of peace of mind in your retirement years. It would feel pretty good, don't you think?

So many people lost a lot of sleep during that time. So many people didn't retire as planned, or those who did, were stressed about being able to maintain their standard of living in retirement. Luckily, my mom didn't have to worry about a thing, all because she placed a good portion of her hard-earned money into Fixed Index Annuities.

And you know what's even better?

When the market started going back up, my mom's money started growing from where it had locked in. While everyone was fighting to catch up and get back to where they were before the crash, my mom was already ahead of the game. (Perhaps it's inappropriate for me to use the term "game" here. The Safety and Security of your retirement money and income is no Game at all!)

This can be a very powerful strategy for *part* of your money. We say part of your money because this tool is typically best reserved for *a portion* of your money, not *all* of it. Generally, fixed index annuities are best used for qualified money because your qualified money is already going to be taxable when you take it out (the growth of annuity is taxable).

In strategic planning, you want to not just look at the assets, but you want to see how those assets are affected by taxation, or how those assets fit into the taxation of another vehicle. Qualified money (IRA, 401(k), 403(b), etc.) harmoniously fits with an annuity from a taxation point of view. It's simply an IRA rollover. You won't have any tax consequence.

Guaranteed Income or Safe, Consistent Growth?

There are two types of fixed index annuities: the type that is engineered for the highest guaranteed income, and the type that is engineered for safe, consistent growth.

I know we all want to have our cake and eat it too, but there isn't a financial vehicle out there that can give you everything. We will always have to give up one thing for another. (No sugar coating here . . . I will always tell you like it is!)

The insurance company can't give you everything. They can't give you the complete safety of principal, the most guaranteed lifetime income and the highest opportunity for internal growth in the same vehicle.

Fixed Index Annuity:
Highest Guaranteed Lifetime Income

Pros: From day one, you know exactly what your guaranteed lifetime income will be.

Cons: An internal rate of return that may not be attractive, giving you fewer options later on.

Fixed Index Annuity: Safe, Consistent Growth

Pros: It provides safe, consistent growth and complete protection of principal. It provides more options as time moves forward. You can also create a withdrawal strategy to take money out with confidence (like my mom). I enjoy creating advanced strategies to enhance different financial tools for my clients' benefit. You also have a greater opportunity to leave money behind for your family, which for some is very important.

Cons: The guaranteed amount of income, if you have a rider on this type, may not provide the highest guaranteed lifetime income.

There are pros and cons to everything. They're all a little bit different. It all depends upon your personal situation. For some, it's better to have the type that is engineered for safe, consistent growth, like my mom's annuities are.

My job is to learn what's important to you, learn what you're looking to achieve, where your assets are, and what strategies are best for you in your personal situation. If you are over 50 and want a portion of your money Safe and Secure, an annuity might be part of a wise financial strategy for you.

The Path to Prosperity

What's important to you? What are your goals?

In retirement, we always talk about how much money we have or income that we can count on.

From a financial planning perspective, we want to make certain that you have a strong foundation of income. We want to use the least amount of assets to create the most amount of guaranteed income. That creates more freedom and flexibility for the growth of your other dollars, and the foundation of a comprehensive plan, of protected guaranteed income, that you can count on.

Ultimately, you should be able to reach this path to prosperity so that you can do the things that you want in your life. You can live the lifestyle you want and ultimately be able to leave a legacy to your family or give to a charity, if that's important to you.

All these years, my mother's money has been protected. Thanks to her fixed index annuities, she has never suffered market losses and has had the stability and consistency of income she needed. Most of all, she has had the peace of mind she so richly deserves.

That's what my practice will help you do. My practice will create a comprehensive, Safe and Secure strategic plan, tailored to relieve Retirement Anxiety and Compound your Wealth no matter what the Market does.

Chapter Fourteen:

Are Your Gains Locked In?

In the next chapter, I'm going to introduce powerful, tax-advantaged strategies, but first...

We just spent an entire chapter talking about the benefits of annuities. I also spent quite a bit of time stressing the importance of *goals* and *strategies* over specific tools, but I'm sure some of you still aren't convinced that this tool can help relieve you of *Retirement Anxiety*, no matter what the market does.

Let's see if learning the following information can help you along... After all, the proof is in the pudding.

As you most of you know, we are on a historic, 9-year Bull Market Run.

People feel good and are happy with their gains . . . but are your market gains **Locked In**?

No, of course not.

When the market eventually takes a turn for the worse, your account will go down. You will lose money.

Let's just hope it won't be as bad as 2008.

But what if you could Lock In your gains?

Let's look at the chart below:

From 01/31/2007 to 01/31/2018

End of Year	Account Value	Return	Account Value	Return
0	1,070,000	N/A	1,000,000	N/A
1	1,070,000	0.00%	599,093	-40.09%
2	1,180,510	10.33%	778,985	30.03%
3	1,326,183	12.34%	932,951	19.76%
4	1,326,183	0.00%	952,022	2.04%
5	1,473,456	11.11%	1,086,729	14.15%
6	1,597,181	8.40%	1,293,091	18.99%
7	1,726,758	8.11%	1,447,165	11.92%
8	1,726,758	0.00%	1,407,450	-2.74%
9	1,739,254	0.72%	1,653,092	17.45%
10	2,025,705	16.47%	2,048,391	23.91%
Annualized Return	7.31%		7.43%	

This chart is a direct comparison between the S&P 500 from January 30, 2008 to January 30, 2018, and the gains that a Fixed Index Annuity (FIA) crediting strategy had in the same period.

You see the FIA strategy had a return over that period of time of 7.31% and the S&P's return was 7.43%.

So, what's the BIG difference?

The BIG difference is that gains in the S&P will be lost when the market goes down.

Do you remember 2008? Do you remember losing 30% to 40% of your money? Do you remember how long it took to recover?

Was your money compounding then?

Not to mention, we were all younger, with more time on our side, then.

With the FIA strategy, your 7.31% gain is "Locked In" and cannot be lost!

Not to mention, you won't have to wait years to recover losses like you would in the market. Remember, a 30% loss takes a 43% gain to get back to even, and we aren't even counting if you are taking money out at the same time. Your money will compound from where it is locked in!

Let's look at the graph below:

From 01/31/2008 to 01/31/2018

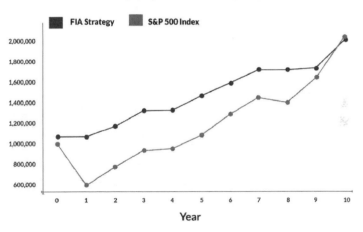

The bottom line represents the S&P and the top line represents the FIA Strategy.

You can clearly see in 2008, when the S&P crashed, and people lost so much money, the top line, the FIA strategy, stayed level. Those people didn't lose any money. Not one penny!

Then you can see as the market started to go up, the FIA strategy went up from where it was locked in each year.

So here we are, at an all-time market high...

Do you think it would be a good idea to "Lock In" your gains and protect yourself from market loss?

Would it be wise to be proactive, and keep your money, knowing that you will have market-like returns without market volatility?

Would that give you more stability, and peace of mind, for your financial life and lifestyle?

For the people who have worked with me to implement this strategy, they have told me it has.

Chapter Fifteen:

How to Avoid the Ticking Tax Time Bomb

Very early on in the book, I reference **Louis D. Brandeis,** a
Supreme Court Justice from 1919 to 1939. His thoughts on
tax avoidance are so powerful, I want to tell you the story, in his
words, again.

"I lived in Alexandria, Virginia. Near the Supreme Court
chambers is a toll bridge across the Potomac. When in a rush, I
pay the toll and get home early. However, I usually drive outside
the downtown section of the city and cross the Potomac on a free
bridge. The bridge was placed outside the downtown Washington,
D.C. area to serve a useful social service: getting drivers to drive
an extra mile to help alleviate congestion during rush hour. If I
went over the toll bridge and through the barrier without paying
the toll, I would be committing tax evasion. However, if I drive
the extra mile outside the city of Washington and take the free
bridge, I am using a legitimate, logical and suitable method of
tax avoidance, and I am performing a useful social service by
doing so. For my tax evasion, I should be punished. For my tax

avoidance, I should be commended. The tragedy in life is that so few people know that the free bridge even exists."

Relieve Retirement Anxiety

If your goal is to Relieve Retirement Anxiety, locking in your gains with an annuity (no matter what the market does) is a terrific solution that may work well for some of you.

But what about a retirement account with tax-free income? For some of you, that may be a more important goal. (Judge Brandeis was onto something.)

Like we've talked about, it's not a question of what the tool is, it's a question of strategy . . . and some people are looking for a strategy to help them diversify their tax portfolio.

In my opinion, tax diversification is something we should *all* consider adding to our financial plan. Earlier in this book, we talked about where taxes are headed, and almost all experts agree that taxes in the future will have to go up. It's simple mathematics.

Ten thousand baby boomers are retiring every day, cashing checks from Social Security and Medicare. And, the population is living longer and getting older, meaning not only do the payments have to last longer, but there are fewer working adults to supplement them.

The government will have to pay for this. How do you think they will be able to do that?

We're already in a multi trillion-dollar deficit . . . so what's going to happen?

Eventually, regardless of which political party is in governmental power, taxes will have to go up, and almost everyone I talk to agrees that will most likely happen.

A Ticking Tax Time Bomb

Most financial goals revolve around protecting and growing wealth. I want to help your Wealth to Compound, and one of the best ways to do that is to protect it from the threat of future taxes.

Like I mentioned earlier in the book, the nationally respected CPA and author, Ed Slott, believes taxes are the "Single biggest threat" to retirement planning. We can't foresee the future, but if taxes do indeed go up, he could very well be right.

Currently, we're in a historically low tax rate . . . and the government just lowered the tax rates even more!

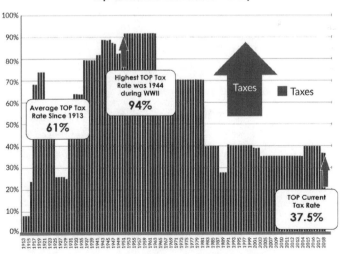

Top US Federal Tax Bracket History

Sure, the rates are low now, but we know that won't last forever. As you can see above, in 1942, taxes were in the 90th percentile for the wealthiest Americans. I don't know how likely it is that we will see tax rates that high again, but we really don't know, do we? The government has the power to change the tax rate at any time, and if they need the money, don't you think they will?

So, what does that mean for your retirement?

If you have a bulk (or all!) of your savings in a qualified, tax-deferred account, it could mean you'll end up giving a lot more of your money in taxes than you expected to Uncle Sam.

Like we've already talked about, throughout our working years, we earn income and we pay tax on our earned income. Most of us put our retirement savings into qualified accounts, where money is contributed *before* taxes are taken out. That money then grows within that qualified account, but the money is tax-deferred, meaning you still owe taxes on it.

When it comes time to retire, and you need to start withdrawing that money, you will owe taxes on that money, not just the money you contributed originally, but the money that you earned through account growth, as well.

Think about it for a moment...

Would you rather pay a small amount of tax on the seed, or a larger amount on the entire harvest?

If you pay on the harvest and defer taxes, and taxes go up like they inevitably will, the money in your tax-deferred retirement account (401(k)s, IRAs, 403(b)s, etc.) is at risk! It's a ticking tax time-bomb!

> If you want to build a solid foundation that will support your Compounded Wealth, you need to diversify your tax portfolio. A percentage of your money should be in qualified accounts and non-qualified accounts. You should have a portion of your money in a tax-free account.

Why You Shouldn't Love Your Roth IRA Account

Some of you are thinking, "Yes, that's why I have my Roth IRA," and singing its tax-advantaged praises.

More and more people are talking about Roth IRAs because they realize taxes will be going up. They want their retirement strategy to include tax-free income.

Many people know about Roth IRA accounts because they allow you to grow retirement income, tax-free. Instead of contributing money pre-tax, you pay the tax first. This helps protect against tax-risk, right?

But the Roth IRA has its own limitations. Because it's a government account, you're limited to only $6,500 a year in contributions. You're also subjected to market volatility (Roth IRA accounts are tied to the market). Lastly, similar to a 401(k) or 403(b), these accounts have limited liquidity; if you withdraw the money too early, you're penalized.

A Roth IRA account can potentially mitigate some tax risk, but that's pretty much its only benefit.

And because it's tied to the market, the money is subjected to market volatility, meaning you could lose a very large portion of your savings.

What's the point of tax-advantaged growth if you lose the majority of your money in the next market crash?

What is a Leveraged Loan?

Roth IRA accounts may be a good tool for some, but for my clients (and me) there's another tool that has proven to work much better.

First and foremost, it gives you tax-advantaged growth. I can't stress the importance of that enough. But unlike your Roth IRA account, this tool gives you access to tax-free income through the use of **leveraged loans**, allowing you to keep your Wealth Compounded no matter what the market (or government) does.

What's a leveraged loan?

It's a loan secured with a lien on an asset or assets.

Many of my clients who are real estate investors understand this concept well.

Think about your house. If you owe a mortgage on your house, you agree to pay the bank the amount you owe. You have borrowed money to pay for the house, and as you pay down that mortgage, the value of your house continues to grow (in most cases). The money you owe the bank has no effect on the value of the house.

Leveraged loans are very similar.

Look at this as an example.

If you had a savings account of $100,000, and then took out $40,000, you would only be earning money on the $60,000 you have left.

But let's say you borrow from your $100,000 cash-value Wealth Compounded Life Insurance instead of your savings account. The life insurance company uses your Death Benefit as collateral, and even though you have borrowed $40,000, you still earn interest/dividends on $100,000. Yes, the insurance company will charge you interest on the loan, but it is a *leveraged* loan.

If you are younger, this works as your own private banking system. (I can tell you more about his concept in person.)

For those of us who will use this for tax-free supplemental retirement income, you will never pay the money back and the leverage creates income you can count on.

It serves us in both purposes very well.

Tax-Advantaged Growth... And So Much More!

What tool could I possibly be talking about?

Strategically designed, Wealth Compounded Life Insurance!

Not only does it allow for tax-advantaged account growth, and tax-free income, it also permits the use of leveraged loans to ensure your Wealth Compounds.

You're probably thinking, "That can't be right."

But I assure you, it is.

The most unique feature of permanent life insurance is that under Section 72 of the Internal Revenue Code, the accumulation of cash inside the insurance contract is tax advantaged.[43] Many of America's wealthy have used this strategy for years!

Section 72(e) and 7702

The most unique feature of permanent life insurance is that under Section 72(e) and 7702 of the Internal Revenue Code the accumulation of cash inside the insurance contract is tax advantaged. Not only can the cash value accumulate tax free, but the cash can also be accessed tax free.

Hence, the living benefit of life insurance: It is a unique vehicle that allows tax free account value accumulation, allows you to access your money tax free, and, when you die, blossoms in value and transfers income tax free!

If you're looking for a tax-advantaged strategy to accomplish your financial goals, Wealth Compounded Life Insurance (WCLI) very well may be the answer.

But seek the guidance of someone who is an expert at engineering the policy for *your* benefit . . . not the benefit of the insurance company.

These types of policies must be strategically designed for *your* benefit, *not* the benefit of the agent or the life insurance company itself.

Too many financial planners either don't know how or are unwilling to structure the policies to your benefit.

(Can you guess the reasons why?)

And believe it or not, tax-advantaged growth isn't the only benefit to WCLI. In the next chapter, I'm going to tell you what those other benefits are and how a Wealth Compounded Life Insurance policy should be properly structured.

Chapter Sixteen:

Can You Throw Your Preconceived Notions Out the Window?

If I can show you how you how to possibly increase your retirement income by 25-40%, without having to reduce your lifestyle, would you be interested?

A week ago, a new client walked into my office. He is 70 and just relocated to Southern Florida from New Jersey.

Throughout his working life, he acquired quite a bit of wealth, but he had recently gone through a divorce and had to give away a substantial number of his assets. Over the past five years, his business also hadn't been performing well, so he was concerned about having enough money to live off in retirement.

We sat down and looked at all his accounts...and I was pleasantly surprised by what I saw. For decades, he had been contributing to a life insurance policy and had over $800,000 of cash value accumulated. When I explained to him that the money was tax-free, AND he could borrow against it to supplement his retirement income, he was ecstatic. He went on to tell me that years ago, when he had his business, someone presented the CVLI to him and told him then, "This will be one of the best investments you ever make." And now he realized he was right! He had come into my office very stressed out but learning that he had enough money to live off, he was instantly relieved.

He was also grateful to know the decision he made years ago was the right one because it had provided him with tax-free retirement income today.

Your Preconceived Notions

In the last chapter, I talked about the importance of tax diversification. I also showed you that one of the best places to grow your wealth tax-free is inside a life insurance policy.

Wealth Compounded Life Insurance (WCLI) is a tool, a product that you will soon learn can be used in many different strategies to accomplish a wide variety of goals.

Even though I just showed you the tax-advantaged benefits, I know many of you still aren't convinced the tool has living benefit merits. But before I tell you about the additional living benefits of WCLI, I want to ask you to throw your preconceived notions out the window.

Are you willing to do that for just a bit? After all, we all don't know what we don't know, right?

I want to arm you with knowledge so that you won't miss out on something the wealthy have been benefiting from, on a massive scale (for years), that is now available for most hardworking American families.

Let me ask you this: Do you think the wealthy make financial decisions based on the name of the tool?

No! They evaluate the strategy and the product, then determine whether or not it will fit in with their financial life and help them achieve their goals. The wealthy focus on their *goals*, not the name of the product.

Many of us get caught up in the names of tools and aren't open minded about that product's function.

So, that begs this next question:

"Are you an open-minded person who can look at what an asset does, and not get all tangled up in what it's called?"

If you are, then the asset I'm about to discuss could become a powerful tool in your portfolio.

Life Insurance or Death Insurance?

What if I told you there was a way to leave a legacy, money for your children and grandchildren, without having to reduce your lifestyle in retirement?

Most of us hear "Life Insurance" and think "Death Insurance," with the preconceived notion that it only provides a benefit to our loved ones after we pass...

But like the case with annuities, there are different types of life insurance.

When you think "Death Insurance," you're thinking **term life insurance**, which is a policy most of us get when we're young to protect our families in case of a tragic, early passing.

Term insurance works this way. You pay a rate for 10, 20, or 30 years to an insurance company for a certain amount of death benefit coverage.

If you don't pass away during the allotted 'term' of time, then the life insurance company keeps the money. This is quite profitable for life insurance companies as only about 1-2% of term polices pay a death claim. This means that 98% or more of the term premiums collected stay with the life insurance company.

A term life policy protects your family in case of death, but other types of policies are meant to protect your money *while you're still alive*. One of them is Wealth Compounded Life Insurance.

Like we've already talked about, growth and withdrawals from a WCLI are tax-advantaged because of the IRS Code 72 & 7702, but there are many, many benefits.

A Multi-Faceted Financial Device

Picture a smart phone.

Do you have one?

I would say that 95% of us do.

Would you agree? And if you do, would you ever consider getting rid of it?

It's not really a phone anymore. We can use it to make phone calls, sure, but we also use it as a clock, a timer, and an alarm. We use it for GPS, email, and TV. More people take pictures on an iPhone everyday than any other camera! Personally, I'm surprised how often the flashlight feature comes in handy for me. For goodness sake, it is a computer in our hand.

We can certainly use it to call someone, but who really wants to do that anymore? These days, people don't want to be called on the phone, they want text messages.

"How dare you call me without texting first!"

Right?

The Phone is Not Just a Phone Anymore...

It's all of this...

- Clock
- Timer
- Stopwatch
- Alarm
- GPS
- Flashlight
- E-mail
- Text Messages
- Video Recorder
- Audio Recorder
- Television
- Facetime
- Bank
- Wallet
- Games
- Check Weather
- Etc...

But it is called a "Phone" ...

We have a multi-faceted computer device in our pockets (or our purses) at all times, so why not utilize the multi-faceted financial tool that's available to us?

Wealth Compounded Life Insurance is a multi-faceted financial vehicle. It provides you with:

- <u>Tax-advantaged growth (can I mention to you one more time that it provides *tax-free retirement income you can count on*?)</u>

- Safety from market losses

- Locked-in growth

- A private banking system

- Liquidity, use, and control of YOUR money

- Litigation protection

- Transaction privacy

Are those benefits that you would like in a financial tool?

Protection from Market Downturns?

What about a retirement strategy that safeguards your money from market crashes? Protecting yourself from the downturns of the market, over the course of time, makes a significant difference to your overall financial health.

How would you like a financial tool that helps you do that?

No, I'm not talking about a bank account, I'm talking about Wealth Compounded Life Insurance!

> WCLI is structured so that it grows when the market grows but stays the same when the market crashes.

When your money is in a WCLI policy, you don't lose it when the market crashes. It's safe. When the market grows, so does your money.

You can lock in double-digit returns in good years and be confident to never lose money in the bad ones.

Instead of "Selling Low"...

Not only is our life insurance money safeguarded against market losses, we can also use it to protect *ourselves* when the market crashes.

Let me explain.

If you're in retirement and the market goes down, you have options. Instead of "selling low" and withdrawing money from your brokerage account, you can borrow against your life insurance policy without having to worry about losing money.

WCLI policies protect your principal, lock in your gains, and capture those gains, gains that go up from there each year.

We Need A Strategy To Help Deal With Volatility

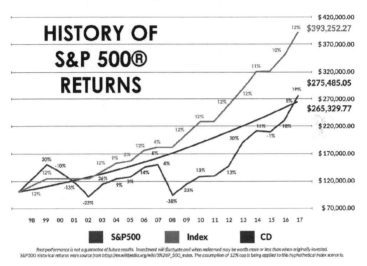

Past performance is not a guarantee of future results. Investment will fluctuate and when redeemed may be worth more or less than when originally invested. S&P500 historical returns were source from https://en.wikipedia.org/wiki/S%26P_500_Index. The assumption of 12% cap is being applied to this hyphothetical index scenario.

Our ability to never lose money within a life insurance product is extremely powerful. While everyone is struggling to catch up after a market crash, we're already ahead of the game, earning gains on money we never lost. (Again, our money is no Game, this is serious stuff.)

Liquidity, Use, and Control

When I was too sick to work, the cash value of my Wealth Compounded Life Insurance policy gave me liquidity, use, and control over my money. I cannot stress enough how much I believe in the importance of this.

I didn't work much for two years, but it was really in that first year that I realized liquidity, use, and control is not only important, it's crucial. Frankly, it's a Financial Lifesaver!

I was able to access my cash value without the concern of having to pay it back until I wanted to. What if I hadn't been able to access that cash? Would we have lost our home, our cars?

Being able to access your cash for emergencies is life-changing.

It took me years to fully recover, but I did recover and eventually, went back to work full-time. I don't know if I'm stronger than ever, but I do know that I am wiser than ever, and I do know that my life would be very different today if I hadn't been able to access the cash inside my WCLI policy.

Is Your 401(k) a Money Trap?

Does your 401(k) give you liquidity, use, and control? What about your IRA? What about your Roth accounts?

Money stored inside a qualified account, for the most part, isn't accessible without paying hefty fees. If an emergency arises, and they absolutely have to take money out, not only are you going to be taxed on the money you withdraw, you'll pay a 10% penalty if you withdraw the money before you turn 59 1/2.

Not only that, but they also lose the opportunity to continue to earn money in the market because they had to take it out.

Most people who are in the accumulation phase of their life, put their money in 401(k)s and IRAs, and have no liquidity, use, or control of their money.

Litigation Protection

Here's another benefit of WCLI: litigation protection.

In most states, the cash inside your WCLI policy is protected from litigation. The death benefit is protected, too.

That may be one of the reasons why physicians place significant amounts of money into their WCLI policies . . . and in the litigious country we live in, that's a concern for many of us.

Your Personal Banking System

Wealth Compounded Life Insurance can work as your personal banking system, allowing you to create leveraged loans, and gives you liquidity, use, and control (more on that later). Some even have long-term care or chronic illness riders, as well as transaction privacy. (I'm a really big believer in **transaction privacy**.)

If you borrow money from the bank or get a credit card, etc., it's reported to the major credit bureaus.

That isn't the case with insurance companies. Any transactions between you and the life insurance company, borrowing money, paying it back, etc., is completely private between you and the life insurance company. Aside from the fact that we just had that horrible Equifax issue with people's information being stolen, in today's environment, transaction privacy is a big deal.

A Maximum Living Benefits Policy

There are many, many benefits to WCLI . . . but only if the policy is properly structured.

First and foremost, A WCLI is structured for maximum living benefits.

I think this is easier to visualize with an example.

Let's suppose you have a $500,000 **death benefit**. There's a *minimum* that you <u>have</u> to pay for that death benefit. There's also a *maximum* that you <u>can</u> pay for that death benefit.

Who determines the minimum?

The insurance companies. (Most people know that.)

Who determines the maximum?

A lot of people don't know the IRS determines the maximum.

Well, let me ask you a question: Why does the IRS care how much money you put into a life insurance policy?

Because the money inside a WCLI policy grows tax-deferred and can be accessed tax-free.

For years, the rich have been using life insurance as a tax haven. Before he died, Malcom Forbes bought the maximum amount of life insurance he could, almost every year. The majority of the company's income was used to purchase "Enormous sums of life insurance".

Why?

Because they want to control the amount of taxable (versus tax-advantaged) benefits you can have and the cash value of the insurance policy grows tax-deferred and can be accessed tax free!

What we want to do is make a **maximum living benefits policy**, and by doing that we're putting <u>more</u> money into the policy than the insurance company requires for the death benefit (that minimum we just talked about).

By putting more money into the policy that the insurance company requires, we are minimizing the expenses, which enhances the tax-advantaged living benefits.

When we lower the expenses, what does that mean to you and to your cash value?

Most people get this answer right.

<u>You get better tax-deferred cash accumulation and more tax-free income. Your Wealth Compounds better and faster!</u>

When we create a Living Benefits policy, the cash value grows tax-free. It's also protected against market losses and is *accessible*, meaning you can easily get a hold of your money, without penalty.

When structuring a WCLI, you need to make sure to include the following:

Wealth Compounded Life Insurance Benefits:

- Maximum Living Benefits
- Tax-Deferred Wealth Compounded Life Insurance Growth
- Tax-Free Wealth Compounded Life Insurance Withdrawals
- Protection from Market Volatility
- Liquidity, Use and Control of Your Money
- Being Your Own Banker
- Transaction Privacy
- Optional Chronic & Long-Term Illness Benefits

Can You Live without Your Cell Phone?

Wealth Compounded Life Insurance provides absolute security because it becomes your financial foundation.

Remember that smart phone?

A WCLI is multi-faceted because it protects your money from any type of market loss, grows tax-advantaged, locks in your gains, provides liquidity, tax-free retirement income, and has a tax-free death benefit. It also gives your other dollars more freedom and flexibility to weather different storms (market volatility, taxes, etc.).

Future Strategic Options

If you're in retirement and you have had a big loss in the market, you can take out more money from your WCLI while your other money regains its value. This is possible because you haven't lost money in the policy, you're simply taking a leverage loan against that money, meaning that money continues to grow.

What if your health has changed as you've gotten older? You can decide to allow the cash inside your living benefits WCLI policy to grow because your death benefit will continue to grow with it. You can use the taxable money from your market accounts to live on because you have the protection of the Tax-Free death benefit for your family.

Is Wealth Compounded Life Insurance Right for You?

Wealth Compounded Life insurance saved my financial life. I'll tell you all about it in the last chapter of the book, but in short, when I couldn't work because of health issues, the cash value inside my WCLI policy provided me with income. I really don't know what I would have done without it.

But just because life insurance was (and still is) right for me, doesn't mean it's right for you. My goal is to provide my clients with what is best for them. For some, it might be an annuity or Wealth Compounded Life Insurance, but it might not.

Just the other day, I was working with a client who wanted to put $2,800 a month into his Wealth Compounded Life Insurance policy. We started talking about where the money was coming from and come to find out he had two kids on track to enter college within 3-6 years. Putting $2,800 a month into an insurance policy meant diverting $800 from his kids' college savings plans.

I looked at him and didn't blink. I was very serious.

I said, "You can't do that. You're too close to when your kids are going to go to college. It doesn't make sense to put that money in a life insurance policy because you need a bigger timeline."

"What do you mean?" He asked. He crinkled his nose, confused.

"Look, I will make more money if you move that $800 into your life insurance policy, but if you do, you're not going to get the desired effect in a short period of time. You need to start withdrawing money in three years, which could hurt your policy. You're better off putting the money in a savings account at the bank."

Now it was his turn to stare at me.

"Don't do it. I'll make less money, but I'm giving you the right advice."

Yes, like anyone in business, I need to make a living, but what I suggest has to be what's right for you. Since my youth, it has been my goal to help people. I want to be somebody that looks at the big picture and helps people make the best possible decision for their unique situation.

Is Wealth Compounded life insurance right for you?

Maybe.

If you're ready to find out, visit www.WealthCompounded. com to schedule a complimentary consultation.

But, maybe you're still not convinced.

Maybe you're asking,

"Why haven't I heard about this before?"

In the next chapter, I can tell you one of the main reasons why...

Chapter Seventeen:

The Truth About Unbiased Financial Advice

In the last chapter, I told you about the client from New Jersey who had $800,000 of cash value inside his life insurance policy.

After meeting with me, he paid a financial advisor specializing in the market a visit.

Do you know what that advisor told my new client to do with the $800,000 of Cash Value in his policy?

He told him to cash it out and invest the full amount in the market!

When my client told me the story, I was flabbergasted. I couldn't believe it. Here I was, telling my client he could use that $800,000 to support his lifestyle in retirement, yet another advisor was telling him to risk it all in the market!

Why was that advisor telling him to cash out his policy? Because that advisor works for a company (you would certainly know the name if I mentioned it) that only works with people's money at risk in the market.

Everyone is different, and we need to tailor strategies to your unique goals. But no matter what you need, and no matter who you ask, the truth is, there's no such thing as unbiased financial advice . . . and I won't give it to you, either.

If you work with an advisor who works for a large company (Morgan Stanley, Edward Jones, Merrill Lynch, Chase Bank, MassMutual, New York Life, etc.), then he or she is being directed to sell that company's financial products and strategies. That advisor is limited to what he or she can offer you.

Maybe you haven't been offered a life insurance product because your financial advisor isn't permitted (or directed) to do so.

That isn't a disparagement. No one is trying to hide it. There are plenty of fine, high-quality people at each of those institutions. But from a business perspective, *of course* they have to use their company's recommended products . . . which means they are limited in what they can actually do and what they can offer you.

I came in to the business through one of those institutions. I was directed to sell the company's financial products and strategies.

But I was uncomfortable because I felt limited. I didn't like having to find only the right square-pegged client to fit inside their square hole. Therefore, I opened my own practice, Safe Secure Financial, and became an independent advisor.

Now, just because I'm no longer beholden to any specific financial institution, doesn't mean I don't have my own biases.

Of course, I do.

I have my own biases because I'm a human being!

Everyone is biased. We *all* have our own opinions. A Money Manager's bias is to have your money in the market. A CPA's bias is to save you taxes that year. My bias is toward Safe and Secure financial planning. People who desire to protect and grow their money with confidence, could <u>greatly</u> benefit from my bias.

Yes, I believe in a comprehensive plan, and I believe in a foundation of protecting my clients' money, and never losing it. I want my clients to have the peace of mind of knowing their money will not just be there but be there when they need it!

The Series 65 License

Back to my original question: "Why haven't you heard of Wealth Compounded Life insurance?"

Some advisors simply don't have insurance products to offer . . . and others aren't even aware they exist!

Maybe this story will help to explain.

A few years ago, I was studying for the Series 65 exam. A Series 65 is a securities license for an investment advisor and covers the regulations and rules of the field. It's one of the most sought-after licenses in today's financial field.

The exam is 180 minutes long, and the study guide is very comprehensive, covering nearly 700 pages. It talks about stocks, bonds, mutual funds, ETFs, options, taxation, and every different type of financial instrument and strategy.

As I studied, I got to the chapter in the book where it talked about annuities. I consider myself an expert in annuities and thought the chapter would be easy. Of course, academics are a little bit different than the real world, so there was some nuance, but overall the chapter was familiar.

Then it came to the life insurance part of the book. Again, *this is my expertise*, I thought, and had no problem going through it.

I got to the paragraph that talks about universal life, how it works, and how it can be structured. At the very bottom, it stated that the policy can be "overfunded." (Yes, the book had overfunded in quotation marks.) This is an advantage because it talks about greatly increasing the policy's cash value and taking out money tax-free.

Finally, as the last line of the paragraph . . . in parentheses...

> *Another use of the flexibility of the premium payments is to "overfund" the policy. That is, pay the premium in excess of those required with that excess going into the savings portion of the policy. This can have the effect of greatly increasing the cash value-money that may be borrowed out of the policy without tax consequences if done properly.*
> *(This is beyond the coverage of this course.[4])*

It was the last sentence in parentheses that irked me. This is the study guide for the Series 65 license exam. This is a very comprehensive financial exam, and yet explaining the overfunded, liquid, and tax-advantaged features of life insurance, is outside the scope of the course?

Everyone Wants Your Money

There is no such thing as unbiased financial advice.

> *(This is beyond the coverage of this course.)*

The Series 65 license exam is the most comprehensive financial test on the market right now . . . and yet in the 700-page study guide, only a tiny, incomplete paragraph is given to a vehicle that greatly increases tax-advantaged growth and tax-free income.

Can you hear the frustration in my voice?

When I first read that, I nearly hit the roof. I'm a pretty mellow guy, but we all have things that get to us, and that really pushed my buttons.

Why do you think cash value life insurance is "Beyond the coverage" of that book?

A securities exam is a Wall Street exam . . . and cash value life insurance isn't a Wall Street product.

Think about it from a business perspective.

Wall Street makes their money when your money is at risk in the market. Their business is to collect assets to put under their management. Do you think they are going to tell you to put your money somewhere they don't make a profit, like a Life Insurance company?

Can you name a product that doesn't charge a fee? Everyone is trying to make a profit. Everyone wants your money.

Wall Street wants your money at risk in the market. They lure you in with the glamour of big returns because they make money when you risk yours. They don't want you to know about Safe and Secure life insurance products because they want *all* your money.

Even what we know about asset diversification favors Wall Street. We've always been told to have a 60/40 or 50/50 market portfolio. And as we get older, we're supposed to start switching over to bonds.

But bonds could lose money in the market as well.

Wall Street doesn't work for insurance companies. They don't make any money selling life insurance policies.

Wall Street wants all your money in Wall Street because that's where they make money...It's their bias!

Marketing Has Distorted Reality

Repetitive marketing has distorted our perception of reality.

I was listening to a keynote speaker at a business conference who was talking about how, in today's world there's a quick fix for everything.

"You want something but can't afford it? Just make three easy installments of $19.95."

"You want to lose weight? Take this miracle pill and shed pounds instantly!"

The same concept applies to financial planning.

"If you invest in *this* hot stock, you can double your money."

Society's repetitive marking has distorted our perception of reality.

> What we really need is a comprehensive financial plan that has a foundation of safety and stability.

However, we get the opposite from Wall Street. Repeatedly, we're told what our "rate of return" will be. Over and over again, we're told that the market will grow your money the fastest because it always does better than any other financial vehicle.

But look at what happened in 2008. The *reality* was that people couldn't retire. The same thing happened in 2000 and 2001. Wall Street products failed, and lives were forever changed.

However, those realities, that *history*, has been forgotten. Wall Street's repetitive, consistent marketing has distorted the perception of the average citizen. They have distorted the reality of average, everyday lives.

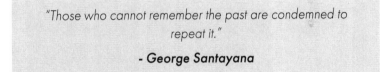

"Those who cannot remember the past are condemned to repeat it."

- George Santayana

Protecting Your Lifestyle

I like talking to people who want to protect their lifestyle. It's not really about protecting your money. Of course, that's important, but it's ultimately about protecting your *lifestyle*.

I'm not interested in repetitive marketing tactics or "get-rich" quick schemes. Like I've told you before, I'm not a one-size-fits-all planner. I believe in educating my clients so they're familiar with all their options. I want to craft a strategy that perfectly fits their individual needs. It isn't about the tools, it's about your goals and the right strategy.

Safe Money Planning is more than simply protecting your money from market volatility and taxes, it's ultimately about protecting your lifestyle.

So, what are you waiting for?

Visit www.WealthCompounded.com to learn more!

Chapter Eighteen:

What's Important About Money to You?

I promised I would tell you the story about how Wealth Compounded Life Insurance saved my financial life...

"There is no substitute for life's experiences."

- Joshua Schlinsky

OK, maybe I can't be credited with that quote . . . but it's something I say often and strongly believe to be true.

As you will recall from the beginning of this book, at the age of 47, I was perfectly healthy one moment, and then, in a fraction of a moment, I suffered a brain hemorrhage.

I didn't have HBP, diabetes, or any other issue that often contribute to such an event; it was just something that happened, and frankly, it was frightening and debilitating. I was unable to feel the left side of my body for quite some time and for months it felt as though someone had literally beaten the crap out of me.

Unfortunately, that was not the only malady I endured over the next two years. It was actually the beginning of a two-year, "multiple health issues odyssey." I have written about it in my book titled, *An Amazing Turn of Events* (It's quite a story!).

It was a very challenging time. It took time, but I am blessed today to be able to feel *much* of the left side of my body and thank God I wasn't permanently crippled. I am very blessed to be alive, to enjoy my life, my family, and to continue to help the people I work with.

During those two years, I was unable to take on new clients. I was not sure when (or if) I would be able to earn a living again. At the time, I had bought my car via a loan on my life insurance policy, because the loan provides leverage, I didn't have to worry about paying it, so I stopped paying myself back.

If I had a loan through Lexus financial, and had stopped paying back the loan, they would have come and picked up my car in the middle of the night!

I was able to borrow from my WCLI policy to have the cash I needed, without the concern of a bank coming after me. I had my own banking system where I was in charge of my money.

> When you need money the most, that is when the bank is the least likely to give it to you. If I had gone to the bank when I was sick and couldn't work, they would have asked how I was going to pay it back. Do you think they would have given me a loan at that time?

Once I recovered and returned to work full-time, I paid "myself" back. I put my money back into my policies while my money was compounding.

And all along, because we created a leveraged loan (like we talked about in the last chapter), the cash was still growing, and is there for my future tax-free retirement income.

Two Very Important Functions

At that point in time, my life insurance policies served two very important functions:

1. The night I had my stroke, I had peace of mind knowing my wife, Lori Beth, would have the financial security she needed.

2. After my stroke, it gave me liquidity and allowed me to use my money as needed, while it continued to grow.

    Remember that old MasterCard commercial with the tag line – "Priceless"?

No Substitute for Life's Experiences

Wealth Compounded Life Insurance helped me survive those two years when I was unable to work full-time. It saved me financially, but it also dramatically helped me emotionally.

My illness, and everything I had gone through, was stressful enough . . . figuring out how I was going to pay for everything was one stressor that my Wealth Compounded Life Policy helped to alleviate.

It all comes back to having peace of mind. I had the peace of mind of knowing that everything was going to be OK. My bills would get paid and my wife would be taken care of if something terrible happened to me, all because I could access the cash value of my life insurance policy.

You're never as healthy as you are today, and you don't know what tomorrow will bring. Any one of us could suddenly become unhealthy and uninsurable.

I've always been an advocate of liquidity, use, and control. Before I got sick, I used to say,

"Liquidity, use, and control of your money is very important, and there's nothing like Wealth Compounded Life Insurance that allows you the leverage to have that."

I always meant that, I always knew it, and I always felt it . . . but yet when you experience it for yourself, the concept is reinforced so dynamically that it creates a clarity that is hard to define. That clarity, that experience has enhanced my passion to bring these benefits and peace of mind to the people I work with.

I know the true, immeasurable value of Wealth Compounded Life Insurance because I was put in a situation where I was forced to rely on it.

When I first got my life insurance policy, I thought it was primarily for tax-free retirement income and the death benefit (and that is exactly how it has worked and is currently working for me), but through my own life's experiences, I learned it was so much more. I cannot overemphasize the security and safety Wealth Compounded Life Insurance means to the foundation of our financial house, and our peace of mind.

There truly is no substitute for life's experiences.

What's Important About Money to You?

At the end of last October, my wife Lori Beth and I flew to Hartford, Connecticut, rented a car, and drove for ninety minutes to Putney, Vermont.

Over the summer, my oldest son Kyle coordinated a weekend family get together. My wife's only brother and his wife have lived in the rural town of Putney since he moved from New York City in 1994. His two sons, who live on opposite ends of the country, and well as my three sons, their wives, and my two grandchildren, all flew in to join us.

As we get older, and our children grow and move to other areas, it is hard to get together. I am lucky that my oldest son, Kyle, lives only 15 minutes from me, but my youngest son Alex lives in Tampa, and my middle son Dane, who has my most prized family members, my two grandchildren, lives in Ocala, both more than a 4-hour drive away. Getting everyone together is a feat in and of itself.

So Much to Be Grateful For

Where does the time go?

Wasn't it just yesterday that my boys were little kids?

Wasn't it just yesterday that we were playing basketball in the driveway, carpooling to school, and helping with homework?

There is so much to be grateful for. Look at them now. So grown up, married, and successful professionals. *There is so much to be grateful for!*

It wasn't easy, (is life ever easy?) but through it all, we live, we grow and realize the blessings we have in our lives.

In Vermont, we simply relaxed. We went for walks in the woods, went apple picking, and toured all four blocks of bustling, downtown Brattleboro. In the evening, we sat around the large fireplace at my brother-in-law's home and enjoyed each other's company. The world slowed down for a weekend.

People who are retired often tell me, *"I am so busy."*

Seems counterintuitive, doesn't it?

But with cell phones, the internet, work, family, and the hustle bustle of everyday life, most of us are busier than ever. Sometimes we just have to MAKE THE TIME, to step back, look at life and what we have achieved, and just . . . *Be grateful.*

What Are You Waiting For?

Not only am I grateful for my family, but I am also grateful for those who have allowed me to help them build their financial Foundation of Success.

My family is my pride and joy, but my work is my passion.

What is the most important thing about your money to you?

Our ability to enjoy all life has to offer. For me, it's about spending time with my family and spoiling my grandchildren. It's not about how much money I have, it's about knowing I will have the money to continue our lifestyle with the peace of mind I have worked so hard to deserve.

By now, wouldn't you agree?

> *"No one can go back and make a brand-new start, but anyone can start from now, and make a brand-new ending."*

It isn't about what you've done financially up to this point, it's about that you are going to do right now.

"The success of what you're currently doing is based upon the foundation that immediately proceeds it."

In this book, I have provided you with a glimpse into how a foundation of Safe money strategies, Tax efficient strategies, and leverage can provide you with many different benefits, so that you can have a secure, consistent and predictable retirement lifestyle, no matter what the markets do.

It isn't too late to start protecting, growing and leveraging your money. I want to provide you with the guidance that is right for *you in your personal situation.*

The best time to plant a tree
was twenty years ago.
The second best time is now.

If there was ever a time to get started, it's now. Visit www.WealthCompounded.com to schedule your complimentary consultation.

IS YOUR WEALTH COMPOUNDED?

The world is changing!

Just look at our ballooning national debt and the economies of all the nations around the world. It is a tenuous time filled with unprecedented problems.

When the stock market crashes and taxes skyrocket, will your money be protected?

"The success of what you are currently doing is based upon the foundation which immediately precedes it."

You need a Financial Foundation of Success and building one requires the right strategies unique to your position.

What are your financial goals? What's important to you?

I have found that most Americans never stop to ask themselves that question. They think of financial *tools* (like stocks, bonds, and mutual funds) when instead they should be focusing on *strategies* that will help them to achieve those goals.

Do you want a Secure, Consistent, and Predicable Retirement Lifestyle, no matter what the stock market or government does?

If you are waiting for the perfect opportunity to start Compounding your Wealth, the time is now.

To speak with Joshua Schlinsky or one of the *Wealth Compounded* specialists about a complimentary consultation, be sure to visit www.WealthCompounded.com.

ACKNOWLEDGEMENTS

Writing this book has been a project I am so grateful to have accomplished.

Writing a book while working full-time (as well as making sure my family is not ignored) is not an easy task.

My goal is to provide people with information, so they can make a wise decision that is best for them.

I want to thank my lovely wife for her input, and the sacrifices she made for the time needed to research and write this book.

My gratitude also extends to my editor, the guidance of my colleagues, and the proofreaders that helped me to share this book with each and every one of you.

END NOTES

1. Julie Hirschfeld Davis and Michael D. Shear, "Trump Signs Spending Bill, Reversing Veto Threat and Avoiding Government Shutdown" The New York Times (March 23, 2018) https://www.nytimes.com/2018/03/23/us/politics/trump-veto-spending-bill.html (accessed 5.13.18).

2. Anuar D. Ushbayev's Blog, "They are dancing in a room in which the clocks have no hands." (September 2, 2014) https://anuarushbayev.wordpress.com/2014/09/02/they-are-dancing-in-a-room-in-which-the-clocks-have-no-hands/ (accessed 5.13.18).

3. Dana Anspach, "20 Years of Stock Market Returns, by Calendar Year", The Balance (November 28, 2017) https://www.thebalance.com/stock-market-returns-by-year-2388543 (accessed 5.13.18).

4. "Four Percent Rule", Investopedia.com https://www.investopedia.com/terms/f/four-percent-rule.asp (accessed 5.13.18).

5. "Morning Star", https://www.google.com/search?q=what+is+morningstar%3F&oq=what+is+morningstar%3F&aqs=chrome..69i57j0l5.2875j0j1&sourceid=chrome&ie=UTF-8 (accessed 5.13.18).

6. Jordan Lite, "Death on Mount Everest: The perils of the descent", Scientific American (December 10, 2008) https://blogs.scientificamerican.com/news-blog/death-on-mount-everest-the-perils-o-2008-12-10/ (accessed 5.13.18).

7. "The IRS", Share It's Funny https://shareitsfunny.com/the-irs/ (accessed 5.13.18).

8. "You May Think You Will Be In A Lower Tax Bracket Later, But You Don't Know", quotehd.com http://www.quotehd.com/quotes/ed-slott-quote-you-may-think-you-will-be-in-a-lower-tax-bracket-later-but-you (accessed 5.13.18).

9. "A Roth 401(k) Or A Roth IRS Takes The Uncertainty Out Of Predicting The Future", quotehd.com http://www.quotehd.com/quotes/ed-slott-quote-a-roth-401k-or-a-roth-ira-takes-the-uncertainty-out-of-predicting (accessed 5.13.18).

10. David M. Walker, "Commentary: Why your taxes could double", CNN (April 15, 2009) https://www.cnn.com/2009/POLITICS/04/15/walker.tax.debt/ (accessed 5.13.18).

11. Robin Saks Frankel, "How your credit score affects your mortgage rate", bankrate.com (December 14, 2017) https://www.bankrate.com/finance/mortgages/how-credit-scores-impact-your-mortgage-rate-1.aspx (accessed 5.13.18).

12. "Straw that broke the camel's back", Wikipedia https://en.wikipedia.org/wiki/Straw_that_broke_the_camel%27s_back (accessed 5.13.18).

13. John M. Mason, "The Stock Market in 2018", Seeking Alpha (December 19, 2017) https://seekingalpha.com/article/4132743-stock-market-2018 (accessed 5.13.18).

14. Mark Hulbert, "Here's the No. 1 lie the bulls tell you about the U.S. market", MarketWatch (September 6, 2016) https://www.marketwatch.com/story/heres-the-no-1-lie-the-bulls-tell-about-the-us-market-2016-09-06 (accessed 5.13.18).

15. "What Is a 401(k)?" The Wall Street Journal http://guides. wsj.com/personal-finance/retirement/what-is-a-401k/ (accessed 5.13.18).

16. "What is the difference between qualified and non-qualified plans?" Investopedia.com, https://www.investopedia.com/ask/answers/206.asp (accessed 5.13.18).

17. "Publication 571 (01/2018), Tax Sheltered Annuity Plans (4013(b) Plans)", IRS (revised January 2018) https://www.irs.gov/publications/p571 (accessed 5.13.18).

18. "Thrift Savings Plan" TFP", Investopedia.com, https://www.investopedia.com/terms/t/thrift_savings_plan.asp (accessed 5.13.18).

19. "SEP Plan FAQs", IRS https://www.irs.gov/retirement-plans/retirement-plans-faqs-regarding-seps (accessed 5.13.18).

20. "What is a Traditional IRA?" Charles Schwab https://www.schwab.com/public/schwab/investing/retirement_and_planning/understanding_iras/traditional_ira (accessed 5.13.18).

21. "SIMPLE IRA Plan", IRS https://www.irs.gov/retirement-plans/plan-sponsor/simple-ira-plan (accessed 5.13.18).

22. "457 plan", Wikipedia https://en.wikipedia.org/wiki/457_plan (accessed 5.13.18).

23. Ben Steverman, "Two-Thirds of Americans Aren't Putting Money in Their 401(k)", (February 21, 2017) Bloomberg https://www.bloomberg.com/news/articles/2017-02-21/two-thirds-of-americans-aren-t-putting-money-in-their-401-k (accessed 5.13.18).

24. "What Is a 401(k)?" The Wall Street Journal http://guides. wsj.com/personal-finance/retirement/what-is-a-401k/ (accessed 5.13.18).

25. Melissa Phipps, "The History of the Pension Plan", The Balance

(April 12, 2018) https://www.thebalance.com/the-history-of-the-pension-plan-2894374 (accessed 5.13.18).

26. Kathleen Elkins, "A brief history of the 401(k), which changed how Americans retire", CNBC (January 4, 2017) https://www.cnbc.com/2017/01/04/a-brief-history-of-the-401k-which-changed-how-americans-retire.html (accessed 5.13.18).

27. Scott Tong, "Father of modern 401(k) says it fails may Americans", MarketPlace.org (June 13, 2013) https://www.marketplace.org/2013/06/13/sustainability/consumed/father-modern-401k-says-it-fails-many-americans (accessed 5.13.18).

28. Kathleen Elkins, "A brief history of the 401(k), which changed how Americans retire", CNBC (January 4, 2017) https://www.cnbc.com/2017/01/04/a-brief-history-of-the-401k-which-changed-how-americans-retire.html (accessed 5.13.18).

29. "401(k)", Wikipedia https://en.wikipedia.org/wiki/401(k)#History) (accessed 5.13.18).

30. Scott Tong, "Father of modern 401(k) says it fails may Americans", MarketPlace.org (June 13, 2013) https://www.marketplace.org/2013/06/13/sustainability/consumed/father-modern-401k-says-it-fails-many-americans (accessed 5.13.18).

31. Kathleen Elkins, "A brief history of the 401(k), which changed how Americans retire", CNBC (January 4, 2017) https://www.cnbc.com/2017/01/04/a-brief-history-of-the-401k-which-changed-how-americans-retire.html (accessed 5.13.18).

32. Timothy W. Martin, "The Champions of the 401(k) Lament the Revolution They Started", The Wall Street Journal (January 2, 2017) https://www.wsj.com/articles/the-champions-of-the-401-k-lament-the-revolution-they-started-1483382348 (accessed 5.13.18).

33. Ben Steverman, "Two-Thirds of Americans Aren't Putting Money in Their 401(k)", (February 21, 2017) Bloomberg https://www.bloomberg.com/news/articles/2017-02-21/two-thirds-of-americans-aren-t-putting-money-in-their-401-k (accessed 5.13.18).

34. "Sequence Risk", Investopedia.com https://www.investopedia.com/terms/s/sequence-risk.asp (accessed 5.13.18).

35. Conrad de Aenlle, "Opinion: John Bogle has a warning for index fund investors", MarketWatch.com (June 1, 2017) https://www.marketwatch.com/story/john-bogle-has-a-warning-for-index-fund-investors-2017-06-01 (accessed 5.13.18).

36. "Vanguard S&P 500 ETF", Morningstar http://performance.morningstar.com/funds/etf/total-returns.action?t=VOO (accessed 5.13.18).

37. "Bankruptcy of Lehman Brothers", Wikipedia https://en.wikipedia.org/wiki/Bankruptcy_of_Lehman_Brothers (accessed 5.13.18).

38. Andrew Ross Sorkin, "JP Morgan Pays $2 a Share for Bear Stearns", The New York Times (March 17, 2018) http://www.nytimes.com/2008/03/17/business/17bear.html (access 5.13.18).

39. "Bailed out banks", CNN Money http://money.cnn.com/news/specials/storysupplement/bankbailout/ (accessed 5.13.18).

40. "Bailout litigation", Wikipedia https://en.wikipedia.org/wiki/American_International_Group#Bailout_litigation (accessed 5.13.18).

41. Kimberly Amadeo, "Glass Steagall Act of 1933, Its Purpose and Repeal", The Balance (January 22, 2018) https://www.thebalance.com/glass-steagall-act-definition-purpose-and-repeal-3305850 (accessed 5.13.18).

42. "@6 U.S. Code 72 – Annuities; certain proceeds of endowment and life insurance contracts", Cornell Law School: Legal Information Institute https://law.cornell.edu/uscode/text/26/72 (accessed 5.13.18).

43. "Uniform Investment Advisor Law Exam: Securities License Exam Manual, Series 65", *Kaplan Financial Education*, La Crosse, WI (2011).